BLACK AND WHITE

LAND, LABOR, and POLITICS in the SOUTH

❖—◄◦◦◦◦►—❖

By

TIMOTHY THOMAS FORTUNE

EBONY CLASSICS

❖—◄◦◦◦◦►—❖

Johnson Publishing Company Inc.
Chicago, 1970

Publisher's Note

The Ebony Classics series has been designed for clarity and elegance in the hope of reaching a public outside the research libraries. The text has been entirely reset in a combination of Bodoni typefaces which echo the original editions, but are easier to read. Corrections of typographical errors and inconsistencies of style are the only amendments that have been made.

Other titles currently available in this series are:

The Narrative of Sojourner Truth
Autobiography of a Fugitive Negro by Samuel Ringgold Ward
The Underground Railroad by William Still
My Bondage and My Freedom by Frederick Douglass
Men of Mark by William J. Simmons

Copyright 1884 by T. Thomas Fortune

Reprinted 1970 by Johnson Publishing Company, Inc.
Foreword by John Bracey copyright © 1970

Library of Congress Catalog Card No. 79-102978
SBN No. 87485-030-4
Printed in the United States of America
by the Rand McNally Company
$3.50

FOREWORD TO THE 1970 EDITION

From the 1880's through the opening decade of the twentieth century, T. Thomas Fortune was one of the country's leading journalists and certainly the outstanding black journalist. His political writings marked him as one of the most radical black thinkers of his day. Though his influence diminished after 1907 when he lost control of the New York *Age* to Booker T. Washington, and suffered a nervous breakdown, Fortune was eulogized as the dean of American journalism at the time of his death at the age of 72, in 1928.

Timothy Thomas Fortune was born on October 3, 1856, in Marianna, Jackson County, Florida. His parents, Sarah Jane and Emanuel Fortune, were both slaves, as was T. Thomas for the first nine years of his life. Sarah Fortune died in 1869; Emanuel was active in Reconstruction politics in Florida until he was finally driven from the state. Young Fortune literally grew up in newspaper offices, working at an early age in the office of the *Marianna Courier* and later in the composing rooms of the *Jacksonville-Courier* and the *Daily-Times Union*. He went to school briefly at Stanton School in Jacksonville, but left and took a job as office boy in the Jacksonville post office. He rose to the positions of letter stamper and paper clerk, but left the post office after a disagreement with the Postmaster. In 1874, Fortune received an appointment as agent on the Jacksonville to Chattahoochee mail route. In 1875 his friend Congressman William J. Purnam of the First Congressional District of Florida encouraged his appointment by Secretary B. H. Bristow as Special Inspector of Customs for the Eastern District of Delaware. In the fall of 1875, Fortune enrolled in the Normal Department of Howard University. He remained for approximately two school terms. In 1877 he returned to journalism in the composing room of the *People's Advocate* in Washington, D.C. He married Miss Carrie C.

Smiley this same year. In 1878 Fortune taught in the Florida school system.

In 1879 Fortune went to New York City to advance his journalistic career; in 1880 he edited the *Rumor* which changed its name to the New York *Globe* under the editorship and ownership of Fortune, George Parker and William Walter Sampson. *Black and White*, which presented his radical political and social ideas with candor and clarity, was published in 1884; in November of that year the *Globe* ceased publication, and the New York *Freeman* appeared with Fortune as the sole editor and proprietor. Fortune began writing editorials for Charles A. Dana's New York *Sun*, one of the leading white newspapers in the country, in 1885 and maintained this relationship with the *Sun* for over two decades. In 1886 Fortune published a second book, *The Negro on Politics* in which he elaborated on his strategy of black political independence as typified in the slogan "Race first; then party."

The year 1887 was doubly significant in Fortune's life. First, he combined efforts with Jerome B. Peterson and changed the *Freeman* to the New York *Age*, under which name it became the most popular black paper. Second, Fortune issued a call for the founding of a National Afro-American League which would fight for the political and civil rights of black Americans. It was about this time that Fortune made the acquaintance of Booker T. Washington, forming a close but often stormy friendship that lasted until the sale of the *Age* to Booker T. in 1907.

After three years in which local Afro-American Leagues were formed in over forty cities, Fortune convened a National Afro-American League meeting in Chicago in January 1890. This meeting was attended by 141 delegates from 23 states. Fortune, the temporary chairman, gave the major address and was elected secretary. The presidency went to the less radical Joseph C. Price, president of Livingston College in North Carolina.

Fortune was elected president at the second annual meeting held in Knoxville, Tennessee in 1891. This was a smaller meeting due to hostility from the white press, a lack of funds, and the lack of mass support of black people. By 1893, the League was defunct, but revived as the National Afro-American Council at a meeting in Rochester, New York in 1898. Bishop Alexander Walters was elected president, and Fortune chairman of the executive committee. Booker T. Washington's influence was very much in evidence with the result that the Council meetings often broke down into disputes along pro *vs.* Booker T. lines. Fortune was elected president in 1902 when the Washington faction defeated the W.E.B. DuBois–Ida Wells Barnett faction. Fortune was reelected in 1903, but retired in 1904 after an unsuccessful fund-raising tour. Despite the Council's more respectable public image the black masses still failed to give it support. The Council continued to function though it was weakened by the formation of the Niagara Movement in 1905 and eventually superseded by the NAACP in 1909.

Fortune, during the period of the existence of the Council, worked quite closely with Booker T. Washington on such projects as a test case of the Louisiana Suffrage Law of 1898, and the formation of the National Negro Business League. Fortune supported Washington's views in the pages of the New York *Age* and also wrote occasional speeches for him. By 1903, Fortune and Booker T. were quarreling more and more over questions of political significance as well as over Fortune's personal habits and financial unreliability. Booker T., who had been secretly subsidizing the *Age* for several years, now began to make offers to buy the paper outright. In the fall of 1907, Fortune sold him his interest in the paper. Later in the same year Fortune suffered a nervous breakdown after which he apparently never regained his former vigor.

Fortune continued to write for the New York *Sun* until 1914 when he went to Washington D.C. to establish the short-lived Washington *Sun*. In the 1920's Fortune wrote editorials and gave editorial assistance to the *Negro World*, the organ of Marcus Garvey's Universal Negro Improvement Association. In late 1927 Fortune left the staff of the *Negro World*, moving from his home in Newark, New Jersey to Philadelphia to live under the care of his son Dr. Frederick W. Fortune.

On Saturday, June 2, 1928, T. Thomas Fortune died in St. Marks Hospital in Philadelphia.

Fortune's ideological development can be viewed quite generally in three phases. In the 1880's and early 1890's Fortune applied the ideas prominent among American labor and agrarian radicals in general to the solution of the problems of black Americans. *Black and White* is a stellar example of this phase in Fortune's development. The advocacy of black political independence which rejected rigid adherence to one party or the other, the formation of the National Afro-American League, the use of the newspaper as an instrument of education and agitation, the denunciation of the effects of the increasing monopolization of land and industrial wealth are all characteristic of Fortune's activities in this period. Fortune was attuned to the effects of racism, but did not view it as

a pervasive feature of American culture and therefore optimistically advocated black and white lower class solidarity against the exploitative
white planters and industrial capitalists.

By the late 1890's, with the failure of radical labor and agrarian movements such as the Knights of Labor and the Populists, and the increasingly
severe oppression of blacks epitomized in disenfranchisement, Jim Crow
laws, and lynching, Fortune shifted his emphasis from agitation for political rights to that of group economic development or the bourgeois
nationalism of Booker T. Washington. This shift forms the context of
Fortune's collaboration with Washington in the founding of the National
Negro Business League, the reviving of the Afro-American League, and
the editorial policy of the New York *Age*. Fortune never totally abandoned his advocacy of struggle for political rights and disagreed with
Booker T. over the "Brownsville Episode" of 1906 in which three companies of Negro troops were discharged from the U.S. Army by President Roosevelt for an alleged racial disturbance. Booker T. said that once
the action had been taken there was nothing that could be done and it was
best to keep quiet about it so as not to cause further bitterness and dis-
cord. Fortune, along with all the black press, severely denounced Roosevelt's actions.

After Fortune broke with Booker T. in 1907, he ended his career shar-
ing the mature black nationalism of Marcus Garvey. Little has been
written of this phase of Fortune's career, but it is safe to say that this was
not one in which his general influence was very great.

Fortune published *Black and White* in 1884 at the age of twenty-eight,
his most radical period. The book reflects Fortune's acquaintance with the
ideas of such social thinkers as Karl Marx and Henry George, and is
quite explicit in its condemnation of the evils of capitalism and its advocacy of class struggle. Indeed, Fortune writes:

The primary purpose in publishing this work is to show that the social problems in the South are, in the main, the same as those which afflict every
civilized country on the globe; and that the future conflict in that section will
not be racial or political in character, but between capital on one hand and
labor on the other.... (Author's Preface).

Fortune's vigorous denunciation of racism as a national phenomenon is
a point well made in the opening chapters, but he underestimated the
depth of this racism in American society. The chapter "Condition of
Labor in the South" is quite optimistic about the future, contending that

skin color really would not matter when blacks gained wealth and education, and that the black man, due to his strength and intelligence,

will ultimately turn the tables upon the unscrupulous harpies who have robbed him for more than two hundred years; and from having been the slave of those men, he, in turn, will enslave them. From having been the slave, he will become the master; from having labored to enrich others, he will force others to labor to enrich him. (p. 118-19).

There is little need to point out that this prediction has not yet been born out by history.

The chapters on "Illiteracy—Its Causes" and "Education, Professional and Industrial" effectively relate the problems that befall a nation as the result of a failure to institute mass democratic education. The lack of a well-educated citizenry has affected the nation's political, cultural and economic development. As far as the education of blacks is concerned, Fortune has harsh words for the "missionaries" who came to the post Civil War South to dominate black education. Fortune views their emphasis on theological, classical, and professional training as mistaken and a waste of needed resources. In words that anticipated those of Booker T. Washington at the end of the century, Fortune wrote:

I do not inveigh against higher education; I simply maintain that the sort of education the colored people of the South stand most in need of is *elementary and industrial*. They should be instructed for the work to be done. (pp. 47-48).

On this one question Fortune and Washington did not disagree.

Perhaps the chief contribution of *Black and White* is Fortune's perceptive analysis of the land question in the South. He viewed the lack of ownership of land as the key factor in the failure of blacks as a race to prosper and develop in the South, and further pointed out that the masses of blacks were themselves aware of their situation. Fortune wrote:

For the man who owns the soil largely owns and dictates to the men who are compelled to live upon it and derive their subsistance from it. The colored people of the South recognize this fact. And if there is any one idiosyncrasy more marked than another among them, it is their mania for buying land. They all live and labor in the cheerful anticipation of some day owning a home, a farm of their own. (p. 127).

This nationalistic feeling among the black masses, and the racism of lower-class Southern whites proved to be more decisive in the future developments in the South than any body of common interests and goals among the lower classes of both races. Fortune had held the logical position that these two groups would act in concert. Such a view perhaps reflects Fortune's newspaperman's belief in the power of the printed word.

Fortune was, of course, aware of the possibility that no one would listen to or act upon his views. He spoke of the "spirit of rebellion which will yet shake the pillars of popular government . . . " if the nation does not pursue wiser policies. He also was aware that a people long oppressed might turn to the use of violence and in words that speak to events of the 1960's Fortune wrote that he believed in a "law and order" that should "be predicated upon right and justice," but:

there is another side to be considered, for when injustice wraps itself in the robes of virtue and of law, and calls in the assistance of armies and all the destructive machinery of modern warfare to enforce its right to enslave and starve mankind, what counter warfare can be too savage, too destructive in its operations, to compel attention to the wrong? (p. 97).

Black and White should be read and studied: for its utopian optimism of white and black working-class solidarity as well as for its candid analysis of racism; for its appeal to reason as well as for its understanding that much in American history is unreasonable. T. Thomas Fortune should be lauded for his contribution to black journalism; he should also be lauded for his contribution to black thought. *Black and White* contains a substantial part of that contribution.

JOHN H. BRACEY JR.

Northern Illinois University
DeKalb, Illinois
September, 1969

AUTHOR'S PREFACE

In discussing the political and industrial problems of the South, I base my conclusions upon a personal knowledge of the condition of classes in the South, as well as upon the ample data furnished by writers who have pursued, in their way, the question before me. That the colored people of the country will yet achieve an honorable status in the national industries of thought and activity, I believe, and try to make plain.

In discussion of the land and labor problem I but pursue the theories advocated by more able and experienced men, in the attempt to show that the laboring classes of any country pay all the taxes, in the last analysis, and that they are systematically victimized by legislators, corporations and syndicates.

Wealth, unduly centralized, endangers the efficient workings of the machinery of government. Land monopoly—in the hands of individuals, corporations or syndicates—is at bottom the prime cause of the inequalities which obtain; which desolate fertile acres turned over to vast ranches and into bonanza farms of a thousand acres, where not one family finds a habitation, where muscle and brain are supplanted by machinery, and the small farmer is swallowed up and turned into a tenant or slave. While in large cities thousands upon thousands of human beings are crowded into narrow quarters where vice festers, where crime flourishes undeterred, and where death is the most welcome of all visitors.

The primal purpose in publishing this work is to show that the social problems in the South are, in the main, the same as those which afflict every civilized country on the globe; and that the future conflict in that section will not be racial or political in character, but between capital on the one hand and labor on the other, with the odds largely in favor of nonproductive wealth because of the undue advantage given the latter by the pernicious monopoly in land which limits production and forces population disastrously upon subsistence. My purpose is to show that poverty and misfortune make no invidious distinctions of "race, color, or previous condition," but that wealth unduly centralized oppresses all alike; therefore, that the labor elements of the whole United States should sympathize with the same elements in the South, and in some favorable contingency effect some unity of organization and action, which shall subserve the common interest of the common class.

T. Thomas Fortune.

New York City, July 20, 1884.

CONTENTS

On a summer day, when the great heat induced a general thirst, a Lion and a Boar came at the same moment to a small well to drink. They fiercely disputed which of them should drink first, and were soon engaged in the agonies of a mortal combat. On their suddenly stopping to take breath for the fiercer renewal of the strife, they saw some vultures in the distance, waiting to feast on the one which should fall. They at once made up their quarrel, saying, "It is better for us to be friends, than to become the food of crows or vultures."—*Æsop's Fables*.

protest against an odious tyranny; it did not matter that in the armies of the colonies, in rebellion against Great Britain, there were (according to the report of Adjutant General Scammell), on the 24th day of August, 1778, 755 regularly enlisted negro troops; it did not matter that in the second war with Great Britain, General Andrew Jackson, on the 21st day of September, 1814, appealed to the "free colored people of Louisiana" as "sons of freedom," who were called upon to defend *our* most inestimable blessing," the right to be free and soverign, and to "rally around the standard of the eagle, to defend all which is dear in existence;" it did not matter that in each of these memorable struggles the black man was called upon, and responded nobly, to the call for volunteers to drive out the minions of the British tyrant. When the smoke of battle had dissolved into thin air; when the precious right to be free and sovereign had been stubbornly fought for and reluctantly conceded; when the bloody memories of Yorktown and New Orleans had passed into glorious history, the black man, who had assisted by his courage to establish the free and independent States of America, was doomed to sweat and groan that others might revel in idleness and luxury. Allured, in each instance, into the conflict for National independence by the hope held out of generous reward and an honest consideration of his manhood rights, he received as his portion chains and contempt. The spirit of injustice, inborn in the Caucasian nature, asserted itself in each instance. Selfishness and greed rode roughshod over the promptings of a generous, humane, Christian nature, as they have always done in this country, not only in the case of the African but of the Indian as well, each of whom has in turn felt the pernicious influence of that heartless greed which overleaps honesty and fair play, in the unmanly grasp after perishable gain.

The books which have been written in this country—the books which have molded and controlled intelligent public opinion—during the past one hundred and fifty years have been written by white men, in justification of the white man's domineering selfishness, cruelty and tyranny. Beginning with Thomas Jefferson's *Notes on Virginia*, down to the present time, the same key has been struck, the same song as been sung, with here and there a rare exception—as in the case of Mrs. Stowe's *Uncle Tom's Cabin*, Judge Tourgée's *A Fool's Errand*, Dr. Haygood's *Our Brother in Black*, and some others of less note. The white man's story has been told over and over again, until the reader actually tires of the monotonous repetition, so like the ten-cent novels in which the white hunter always triumphs over the red man. The honest reader has longed in vain for a glimpse at the other side of the picture so studiously turned to the wall.

Even in books written expressly to picture the black man's side of the story, the author has been compelled to palliate, by interjecting extenuating, often irrelevant circumstances, the ferocity and insatiate lust of greed of his race. He has been unable to tell the story as it was, because his nature, his love of race, his inborn, prejudices and narrowness made him a lurking coward.

And so it has been with the newspapers, which have ever been the obsequious reflex of distempered public opinion, siding always with the strong and powerful; so that in 1831, when the "Liberator" (published in Boston by the intrepid and patriotic Garrison) made its appearance, it was a lone David among a swarm of Goliaths, any one of which was willing and anxious to serve the cause of the devil by crushing the little angel in the service of the Lord. So it is to-day. The great newspapers, which should plead the cause of the oppressed and the down-trodden, which should be the palladiums of the people's rights, are all on the side of the oppressor, or by silence preserve a dignified but ignominious neutrality. Day after day they weave a false picture of facts—facts which must measurably influence the future historian of the times in the composition of impartial history. The wrongs of the masses are referred to sneeringly or apologetically.

The vast army of laborers—men, women, and even tender children—find no favor in the eyes of these Knights of the Quill.

The Negro and the Indian, the footballs of slippery politicians
and the helpless victims of sharpers and thieves, are wantonly
misrepresented—held up to the eyes of the world as beings incapable of imbibing the distorted civilization in the midst of
which they live and have their being. They are placed in the attic,
only to be aired when somebody wants an "issue" or an "appropriation."

There are no "Liberators" to-day, and the William Lloyd
Garrisons have nearly all of them gone the way of all the world.

The part played by the ministry of Christ in the early conflict
against human slavery in this country would be enigmatical in
the extreme, utterly beyond apprehension, if it were not matter
of history that the representatives of the Christian Church, in con-
flicts with every giant wrong, have always been the strongest sup-
porters, the most obsequious tools of money power and the political sharpers who have imposed their vile tyrannies upon mankind. They have alternately supplicated and domineered, crawled
in the dust or mounted the house-top, as occasion served, from
Gregory to the Smiths and Joneses of the present time. So that it
has passed into a proverb, that the ministers of the gospel may be
always counted upon to take sides with the strongest party—always seeking to conciliate "King Cotton," "King Corporation,"
"King Monopoly," and all the other "Kings" of modern growth
—swaying, like the reed in the wind, to the powers that be,
whether of tyranny reared upon a thousand years of usurpation,
military despotism of a day's growth, or presumptuous wealth
accumulated by robbery, hypocrisy and insidious assassination.
Instead of leading in the reformation of leviathan wrongs, the
ministry waits for the rabble to applaud before it commends.* It
was not in this manner that the great Christ set the world in mo-
tion, sowed broadcast the dynamite which uprooted long-estab-

* Be thou the first true merit to befriend,
His praise is lost who waits till all commend.

Pope's Essay on Man.

lished infamies, and prepared the way for the ultimate redemption of the world from sin and error.

If the Christian ministry of the United States did at last recognize the demoralization and iniquity of slavery, it was because the heroic band, headed by William Lloyd Garrison, first fired the heart of the people and forced the ministry to take sides with the righteous cause. I speak not of the few heroic exceptions, but of the mass of the American clergy. If in the evangelization of the black man since the rebellion, the ministry have largely furthered the work, they have done so because there were hundreds and thousands of brave men and women ready to give their time and money to the upbuilding of outraged humanity and the cause of Christ. They have simply put in operation movements conceived and nurtured by the genius and philanthropy of others, and no one of them will claim that he has not reaped an abundant pecuniary harvest for his labors. Yet, I would accord to the ministry of the United States full meed of praise for all that they have done as the agents of the humane, intelligent and philanthropic opinions of the times; and, too, there have been good men who fought the good fight simply because the cause was just.

CHAPTER II

White

It is my purpose in writing this work to show that the American Government has always construed people of African parentage to be aliens, not only when the Constitution was tortured by narrow-minded men to shield the cruel, murderous slave-holder in the possession of his human property, but even now, when the panoply of citizenship is, presumably, all-sufficient to insure to the late slave the enjoyment of full manhood rights as a sovereign citizen.

The conflict of law and the moral sentiment of the country has been long and bloody, and the end is not yet. Political parties in this country do not lead, but follow, public opinion. They hang upon the applause of the rabble, and succeed or fail in their efforts to administer the affairs of Government in proportion as they interpret the wishes of the rabble. Not alone do parties defer to the wishes of the illiterate, the "great unwashed" majority, but individuals as well, who prefer to ride upon the wave of success as the champions of great wrongs rather than to go into retirement as the champions of just principles. The voice of the Charmer is all too powerful to be successfully resisted.

Republics have always been fruitful of demagogues. Such vermin find the soil of democratic government the most fertile and congenial for their operations, because the audiences to which they speak, the passions to which they appeal, are not always of the most reflective, humane or enlightened. Demagogues are the parasites of republics; and that our country is afflicted with an abnormal number of them is to be expected from the tentative nature of our institutions, the extent of our territory and the heterogeneity of our vast population.

Under our government all the peoples of the world find shelter and protection—save the African (who was formerly used as a beast of burden and now as a football, to be kicked by one faction and kicked back by the other) and the industrious Chinaman, who was barred out by the over-obsequiousness of the Congress of the nation, in deference to the Sand-Lot demagogues of the Pacific coast, headed by Denis Kearney, because it was desirable to conciliate their votes, even at the expense of consistency and the unity of the Constitution. That great document, while constantly affirmed to be the most broad and liberal compact ever devised for the governance of man, has always been found to be narrow enough to serve the purposes of the slave oligarch and the make-shifts of the party in power; and has always afforded ample shelter and protection to the lazzaroni of Italy, the paupers of Ireland, and the incendiary spirits of other countries, but yet cannot shield a black man, a citizen and to the manor born, in any common, civil or political right which usually attaches to citizenship.

A putative citizen of the United States commits murder in the jurisdiction of a friendly power, and the Chief Executive of fifty millions of people deems it incumbent upon him as the head of the faction to which he belongs to "call the attention of Congress" to the fact, ostensibly in the interest of justice and fair-play, but obviously to court the good will of the American sympathizers of the assassin. While on the contrary, within a few hundred miles of the National capital, an armed mob of citizens shoot down in cold blood a dozen of their fellow-citizens, but the Chief of the Nation did not deem it at all pertinent or necessary to "call the attention of Congress" to the matter. And why? Because, forsooth, the newspapers, voicing the wishes of the rabble and the cormorants of trade, cry down the "Bloody Shirt," proclaiming, with brazen

effrontery, that each State is "*sovereign*," and that its citizens
have a *perfect right* to terrorize and murder one another, if they
so desire. The Bible declares that "Righteousness exalteth a nation; but sin is a reproach to any people." God save the Union!

But such argument is indicative, not only of American politics
but of Caucasian human nature as well—that human nature
which seldom rises above self-interest in business or politics. If
you have abundance of money, the merchant is all accommoda-
tion, the lawyer all smiles; if you have votes that count, politicians cannot be too obsequious, too affable, too anxious to serve
you. But if you simply have common humanity, clothed in the
awful majesty of a just cause, you appeal in vain to the cormorants of trade, the harpies of law, or the demagogues of
power. Unless you are of the salt salty, unless you are clothed
in broadcloth and fine linen, you cannot obtain even a respectful
hearing.

It took the Abolitionists full thirty years to convince the American people, the ministry of Christ included, that slavery was, pure
and simple, a "Covenant with death and an agreement with hell;"
and then, sad to say, they were convinced against their wills. Their
sense of justice had become so obtuse as to wholly blunt the sense
of reason, the brotherly sympathy of a common race-feeling, and
the broad, liberal and just inculcations of Jesus Christ. The nation
was sunk to the moral turpitude of Constantinople; and not even
a John crying in the wilderness could arouse it to a sense of the
exceeding foulness in the midst of which it grovelled, or of the
storm gathering on the distant horizon.

Although the abolition of slavery had been agitated for more
than thirty years, the nation, which was ruled by politicians of
the usual mental caliber, was startled at the defiant shot upon Fort
Sumter—the shot that echoed the downfall of the foulest institution which has sapped the vitality of any modern government, and
that aroused the people to a sorrowful realization that the power
which defied them was strong enough and desperate enough to

stop at nothing short of the disintegration of the American Union. So the nation, still sympathizing with slavery, still playing with a coal of fire, grappled with the monster, feeling itself powerful to crush it in a few short months.

It was not because the people of the nation hated slavery and oppression that they rushed upon the field of battle; no such righteousness moved them: it was because the slave-power, which had for so long dictated legislation and the interpretation of the laws, would tolerate no adverse criticism or legislation upon the foul institution it championed, and appealed from the forum of reason to the forum of treasonable rebellion to enforce the right so long and (I blush to say it!) *constitutionally* conceded to it.

I do not believe that, in 1860, a majority (or even a respectable minority) of the American people desired the manumission of the slave; it is evident, from the temper of the political discussions of that time, that the combination of parties out of which, in 1856, the Republican party was formed, desired to do no more than to confine the institution of slavery within the territory then occupied. There was certainly very little comfort for the black man in this position of the "party of great moral ideas."

The overtures* made by President Lincoln to the slave-power during the first year of the war were all made in the interest of the perpetuation of the Union, and not in the interest of the slave.

His reply to Mr. Horace Greeley, who urged upon him the importance of issuing an emancipation proclamation is conclusive that he was more concerned about the Union than about the slave:

* I, Abraham Lincoln, President of the United States of America, and Commander-in-chief of the Army and Navy thereof, do hereby proclaim and declare * * * that, on the first day of January, in the year of our Lord one thousand eight hundred and sixty-three, all persons held as slaves within any State, or designated part of the State, the people whereof shall be in rebellion against the United States, shall be then, and thenceforward, and forever free; * * * That the Executive will, on the first day of January aforesaid, by proclamation, designate the States and parts of States, if any, in which the people thereof respectively shall then be in rebellion against the United States.—" President Lincoln's *"Conditional"* *Emancipation Proclamation.*

EXECUTIVE MANSION, WASHINGTON,
August 22, 1862

HON. HORACE GREELEY:—*Dear Sir:* I have just read yours of the 19th, addressed to myself through the *New York Tribune.* If there be in it any statements or assumptions of facts which I may know to be erroneous, I do not, now and here, controvert them. If there be in it any inferences which I may believe to be falsely drawn, I do not, now and here, argue against them. If there be perceptible in it an imperious and dictatorial tone, I waive it in deference to an old friend, whose heart I have always supposed to be right.

As to the policy I seem to be pursuing, as you say, I have not meant to leave any one in doubt.

I would save the Union. I would save it the shortest way under the constitution. The sooner the national authority can be restored, the nearer the Union will be the Union it was.

* * * If there be those who would not save the Union, unless they could at the same time *destroy slavery, I do not agree with them.* My paramount object in this struggle *is to save the Union, and is not either to save or to destroy slavery.* If I could save the Union *without* freeing *any* slave *I would do it,* and if I could save it by freeing *all* the slaves I would do it; and if I could save it by freeing some and leaving others alone I would also do that. *What I do about slavery and the colored race, I do because I believe it helps to save the Union;* and what I forbear I forbear because I do not believe it would help to save the Union. I shall do *less* whenever I shall believe what I am doing hurts the cause, and I shall do *more* whenever I shall believe doing more will help the cause. I shall try to correct errors when shown to be errors, and I shall adopt new views so fast as they shall appear to be true views.

I have here stated my purposes according to my view of *official* duty; and I intend no modification of my oft-expressed *personal* wish that all men, everywhere, should be free.

Yours,

A. LINCOLN

Everything—humanity, justice, posterity—was placed upon the sacrificial altar of the Union, and the slave-power was repeatedly and earnestly invited to lay down its traitorous arms, be forgiven, and keep its slaves. With Mr. Lincoln, as President, it was the Union, first, last, and all the time. And he but echoed the prevailing opinions of his time. I do not question or criticise his *personal* attitude; but what he himself called his "view of official duty" was to execute the will of the people, and that was *not* to abolish slavery, at that time.

As the politicians only took hold of the great question when they thought it would advance their selfish interests, they were prepared to abandon it or immolate it upon the altar of "expediency," when the great clouds of treason burst upon them in the form of gigantic rebellion. The politicians of that time, like the politicians of all times, were incapable of appreciating the magnitude of the questions involved in the conflict.

But the slave-power had been aroused. It was not to be appeased by overtures; it wanted no compromise. It would brook no interference inimical to its "peculiar institution." In the Congress of the nation, in the high places of power, it had so long been permitted to dictate the policy to be pursued towards slavery, it had so inoculated the institutions of the government with the virus of its vicious opinions, that, to be interfered with, to be dictated to, was out of the question. It was Ephraim and his idol repeated.

The South forced the issue upon the people of the country. The Southerners marched off under the banner of "States Rights"— a doctrine they have always championed. They cared nothing for the Union *then;* they care less for the Union *now.* The State to them is sovereign; the nation a magnificent combination of nothingness. The State has in its keeping all option over life, individual rights, and property. The spirit of Hayne and Calhoun is still the star that lights the pathway of the Southern man in his duty to the government. He recognizes no sovereignty more potential than that of his State.

Long years of agitation and bloody war have failed to decide the rights of States, or the measure of protection which the National government owes to the individual members of States. We still grope in the sinuous by-ways of uncertainty. The State still defies the National authority; and the individual citizens of the

Nation still appeal in vain for protection from oppressive laws of States or the violent methods of their citizens. The question, "Which is the greater, the State or the Sisterhood of States?" is still undecided, and may have to be adjudicated in some future stage of our history by another appeal to arms.

CHAPTER III

The Negro and the Nation

◆━━━━◖◍◈◗◗◈◍◗◗━━━━◆

The war of the Rebellion settled only one question: It forever settled the question of chattel slavery* in this country. It forever choked the life out of the infamy of the Constitutional right of one man to rob another, by purchase of his person, or of his honest share of the produce of his own labor. But this was the only question permanently and irrevocably settled. Nor was this *the* all-absorbing question involved. The right of a State to secede from the so-called *Union* remains where it was when the treasonable shot upon Fort Sumter aroused the people to all the horrors of internecine war. And the measure of protection which the National government owes the individual members of States, a right imposed upon it by the adoption of the XIVth Amendment† to the Constitution, remains still to be affirmed.

It was not sufficient that the Federal government should expend its blood and treasure to unfetter the limbs of four millions of people. There can be a slavery more odious, more galling, than mere chattel slavery. It has been declared to be an act of charity

---

* Neither slavery nor involuntary servitude, except as a punishment for crime, whereof the party shall have been duly convicted, shall exist within the United States, or any place subject to their jurisdiction.—Art. XIII. Sec. 1 of the Constitution.

† All persons born or naturalized in the United States, and subject to the jurisdiction thereof, are citizens of the United States and of the State in which they reside. No State shall make or enforce any law which shall abridge the privileges or immunities of citizens of the United States; *nor shall any State deprive any person of life, liberty, or property without due process of law, nor deny to any person within its jurisdiction the equal protection of the laws*—XIVth Amendment, Section 1.

to enforce ignorance upon the slave, since to inform his intelligence would simply be to make his unnatural lot all the more unbearable. Instance the miserable existence of Æsop, the great black moralist. But this is just what the manumission of the black people of this country has accomplished. They are more absolutely under the control of the Southern whites; they are more systematically robbed of their labor; they are more poorly housed, clothed and fed, than under the slave régime; and they enjoy, practically, less of the protection of the laws of the State or of the Federal government. When they appeal to the Federal government they are told by the Supreme Court to go to the State authorities—as if they would have appealed to the one had the other given them that protection to which their sovereign citizenship entitles them!

Practically, there is no law in the United States which extends its protecting arm over the black man and his rights. He is, like the Irishman in Ireland, an alien in his native land. There is no central or auxiliary authority to which he can appeal for protection. Wherever he turns he finds the strong arm of constituted authority powerless to protect him. The farmer and the merchant rob him with absolute immunity, and irresponsible ruffians murder him without fear of punishment, undeterred by the law, or by public opinion—which connives at, if it does not inspire, the deeds of lawless violence. Legislatures of States have framed a code of laws which is more cruel and unjust than any enforced by a former slave State.

The right of franchise* has been practically annulled in every one of the former slave States, in not one of which, to-day, can a man vote, think or act as he pleases. He must conform his views to the views of the men who have usurped every function of government—who, at the point of the dagger, and with shotgun, have

---

* The right of citizens of the United States to vote shall not be denied or abridged by the United States, or by any State, on account of race, color, or previous condition of servitude.—XVth Amendment, Sec. 1.

made themselves masters in defiance of every law or precedent in our history as a government. They have usurped government with the weapons of the coward and assassin, and they maintain themselves in power by the most approved practices of the most odious of tyrants. These men have shed as much innocent blood as the bloody triumvirate of Rome. To-day, red-handed murderers and assassins sit in the high places of power, and bask in the smiles of innocence and beauty.

The newspapers of the country, voicing the sentiments of the people, literally hiss into silence any man who has the courage to protest against the prevailing tendency to lawlessness* and barefaced usurpation; while parties have ceased to deal with the question for other than purposes of political capital. Even this fruitful mine is well-night exhausted. A few more years, and the usurper and the man of violence will be left in undisputed possession of

* While I write these lines, the daily newspapers furnish the following paragraph. It is but one of the *waifs* that are to be found in the newspapers day by day. There is always some *circumstance* with justifies the murder and exculpates the murderer. The black always deserves his fate. I give the paragraph:
"SPEAR, MITCHELL Co., N. C., March 19, 1884.—Col. J. M. English, a farmer and prominent citizen living at Plumtree, Mitchell County, N. C., shot and killed a mulatto named Jack Mathis at that place Saturday, March 1. There had been difficulty between them for several months.
"Mathis last summer worked in one of Col. English's mica mines. Evidence pointed to him being implicated in the systematic stealing of mica from the mine. Still it was not direct enough to convict him, but he was discharged by English. Mathis was also a tenant of one of English's houses and lots. In resentment he damaged the property by destroying fences, tearing off weather boards from the house, and injuring the fruit trees. For this Col. English prosecuted the negro, and on Feb. 9, before a local Justice, ex-Sheriff Wiseman, he got a judgment for $100. On the date stated, during a casual meeting, hot words grew into an altercation, and Col. English shot the negro. Mathis was a powerful man. English is a cripple, being lame in a leg from a wound received in the Mexican war.
"A trial was had before a preliminary court recently, Col. S. C. Vance appearing for Col. English. After a hearing of all the testimony the court reached a decision of justifiable homicide and English was released. The locality of the shooting is in the mountains of western North Carolina, and not far from the Flat Rock mica mine, the scene of the brutal midnight murder, Feb. 17, of Burleson, Miller, and Horton by Rae and Anderson, two revenue officers, who took this means to gain possession of the mica mine."
My knowledge of such affairs in the South is, that the black and the white have an altercation over some trivial thing, and the white to end the argument shoots the black man down. The negro is always a "*powerful fellow*" and the white man a "weak sickly man." The law and public opinion always side with the white man.

his blood-stained inheritance. No man will attempt to deter him from sowing broadcast the seeds of revolution and death. Brave men are powerless to combat this organized brigandage, complaint of which, in derision, has been termed "waving the bloody shirt."

Men organize themselves into society for mutual protection. Government justly derives its just powers from the consent of the governed. But what shall we say of that society which is incapable of extending the protection which is inherent in it? What shall we say of that government which has not power or inclination to insure the exercise of those solemn rights and immunities which it guarantees? To declare a man to be free, and equal with his fellow, and then to refrain from enacting laws powerful to insure him in such freedom and equality, is to trifle with the most sacred of all the functions of sovereignty. Have not the United States done this very thing? Have they not conferred freedom and the ballot, which are necessary the one to the other? And have they not signally failed to make omnipotent the one and practicable the other? The questions hardly require an answer. The measure of freedom the black man enjoys can be gauged by the power he has to vote. He has, practically, no voice in the government under which he lives. His property is taxed and his life is jeopardized, by states on the one hand and inefficient police regulations on the other, and no question is asked or expected of him. When he protests, when he cries out against this flagrant nullification of the very first principles of a republican form of government, the insolent question is asked: "What are you going to do about it?" And here lies the danger.

You may rob and maltreat a slave and ask him what he is going to do about it, and he can make no reply. He is bound hand and foot; he is effectually gagged. Despair is his only refuge. He knows it is useless to appeal from tyranny unto the designers and apologists of tyranny. Ignominious death alone can bring him relief. This was the case of thousands of men doomed by the institution of slavery. *But such is not the case with free men.* You cannot oppress and murder freemen as you would slaves: you cannot so insult them with the question, "What are you going to do about it?" When you ask free men that question you appeal to men who, though sunk to the verge of despair, yet are capable of uprising and ripping hip and thigh those who deemed them incapable of so rising above their condition. The history of mankind is fruitful of such uprisings of races and classes reduced to a condition of absolute despair. The American negro is no better and no worse than the Haytian revolutionists headed by Toussaint l'Overture, Christophe and the bloody Dessalaines.

I do not indulge in the luxury of prophecy when I declare that the American people are fostering in their bosoms a spirit of rebellion which will yet shake the pillars of popular government as they have never before been shaken, unless a wiser policy is inaugurated and honestly enforced. All the indications point to the fulfillment of such declaration.

The Czar of Russia squirms upon his throne, not because he is necessarily a bad man, but because he is the head and center of a condition of things which squeezes the life out of the people. His subjects hurl infernal machines at the tyrant because he represents the system which oppresses them. But the evil is far deeper than the throne, and cannot be remedied by striking the occupant of it—*the throne itself must be rooted out and demolished.* So the Irish question has a more powerful motive to foment agitation and murder than the landlord and landlordism. The landlord simply stands out as the representative of the real grievance. To remove *him* would not remove the evil; agitation would not cease; murder would still stalk abroad at noonday. *The real grievance is the false system which makes the landlord possible.* The appropriation of the fertile acres of the soil of Ireland, which created and maintains a privileged class, a class that while performing no labor, wrings from the toiler, in the shape of rents, so much of the produce of his labor that he cannot on the residue support himself and those dependent upon him aggravates the situation. It is this system which constitutes the real grievance and makes the landlord an odious loafer with abundant cash and the laborer a constant toiler always upon the verge of starvation. Evidently, therefore, to remove the landlord and leave the system of land monopoly would not remove the evil. Destroy the latter and the former would be compelled to go.

Herein lies the great social wrong which has turned the beautiful roses of freedom into thorns to prick the hands of the black men of the South; which made slavery a blessing, paradoxical as it may appear, and freedom a curse. It is this great wrong which has crowded the cities of the South with an ignorant pauper population, making desolate fields that once bloomed "as fair as a garden of the Lord," where now the towering oak and pine-tree flourish, instead of the corn and cotton which gladdened the heart and filled the purse. It was this gigantic iniquity which created that arrogant class who have exhausted the catalogue of violence to obtain power and the lexicon of sophistry for arguments to extenuate the exceeding heinousness of crime. How could it be otherwise? To tell a man he is free when he has neither money nor the opportunity to make it, is simply to mock him. To tell him he has no master when he cannot live except by permission of the man who, under favorable conditions, monopolizes all the land, is to deal in the most tantalizing contradiction of terms. But this is just what the United States did for the black man. And yet because he has not grown learned and wealthy in twenty years, because he does not own broad acres and a large bank account, people are not wanting who declare he has no capacity, that he is improvident by nature and mendacious from inclination.

CHAPTER IV

The Triumph of the Vanquished

There are those throughout the length and breadth of our great country who make a fair living by traducing better men than themselves; by continually crying out that the black man is incapable of being civilized; that he is born with the elements of barbarity, improvidence and untruthfulness so woven into his very nature that no amount of opportunity, labor, love, or sacrifice can ever lift him out of the condition, the "sphere God designed him to occupy"—as if the great Common Parent took any more pains in the making of one man than another. But those who utter such blasphemy, who call in the assistance of the Almighty to fight the battles of the devil, are the very persons who do most by precept and example to make possible the verification of their blasphemy. They carry their lamentations into the pulpit, grave convocations, newspapers, and even into halls of legislation, State and Federal. They are the false prophets who blind the eye of reason and blunt the sympathies of honest, well-meaning men. They are the Jonases on board the ship of progress. They belong to that class of men who would pick flaws in the finest work of art. They find fault with the great mass of ignorance around them, contending that the poor victims have only themselves to blame for their destitute and painful condition, and, therefore, are not entitled to the sympathy or charity of their more fortunate brethren—unmindful that the great Master, judging by the false laws of men, declared that "the poor ye have always with you;" while the very rich are held up as monsters of selfishness, rapacity and the most loathsome of social vices. It is, therefore, hardly to be expected that this class of persons would find anything good in the nature of the lately enslaved black man, or any improvement in his condition since a generous Government had made him an ignorant voter and a confirmed pauper—the victim of his former master, to be robbed outright by designing and unscrupulous harpies of trade, and to be defrauded of his franchise by blatant demagogues or by outlaws, to whom I will not apply the term assassins" for fear of using bad English.

When the American Government conferred upon the black man the boon of freedom and the burden of the franchise, it added four million men to the already vast army of men who appear to be specially created to labor for the enrichment of vast corporations, which have no souls, and for individuals, whom our government have made a privileged class, by permitting them to usurp or monopolize, through the accepted channel of barter and trade, the soil, from which the masses, the laboring masses, must obtain a subsistence, and without the privilege of cultivating which they must faint and die.* It also added four millions of souls to what have been termed, in the refinement of sarcasm, "the dangerous classes" †—meaning by which the vast army of men and women

---

* We of the United States take credit for having abolished slavery. Passing the question of how much credit the majority of us are entitled to for the abolition of Negro slavery, it remains true that we have only abolished one form of slavery—and that a primitive form which had been abolished in the greater portion of the country by social development, and that, notwithstanding its race character gave it peculiar tenacity, would in time have been abolished in the same way in other parts of the country. We have not really abolished slavery; we have retained it in its most insidious and widespread form—in the form which applies to whites as to blacks. So far from having abolished slavery, it is extending and intensifying, and we made no scruple of setting into it our own children—the citizens of the Republic yet to be. For what else are we doing in selling the land on which future citizens must live, if they are to live at all.—Henry George, *Social Problems*, p. 209.

† Although for the present there is a lull in the conflict of races at the South, it is a lull which comes only from the breathing-spells of a great secular contention, and not from any permanent pacification founded on a resolution of the race problem presented by the Negro question in its present aspects. So long as the existing mass of our crude and unassimilated colored population holds its present place in

who, while willing and anxious to make an honest living by the labor of their hands, and who—when speculators cry "over-production," "glutted market," and other clap-trap—threaten to take by force from society that which society prevents them from making honestly.

When a society fosters as much crime and destitution as ours, with ample resources to meet the actual necessities of every one, there must be something radically wrong, not in the society but in the foundation upon which society is reared. Where is this ulcer located? Is it to be found in the dead-weight of illiteracy which we carry? The masses of few countries are more intelligent than ours. Is it to be found in burdensome taxation or ill-adjusted tariff regulations? Few countries are burdened with less debt, and many have far worse tariff laws than curse our country. Is it to be found in an unjust pension list? We hardly miss the small compensation which we grant to the men (or their heirs) who, in the hour of National peril, gave their lives freely to perpetuate the Union of our States. Where, then, is secreted the parasite which is eating away the energies of the people, making paupers and criminals in the midst of plenty and the grandest of civilizations? Is it not to be found in the powerful monopolies we have created? Monopoly in land, in railroads, telegraphs, fostered manufactures, etc.,—the gigantic forces in our civilization which are, in their very nature, agents of public convenience, comfort and absolute necessity? Society, in the modern sense, could not exist without these forces; they are part and parcel of our civilization. Naturally, therefore, society should control them, or submit to the humiliation of being ruled by them. And this latter is largely the case at the present time. Having evolved those forces

the body politic, we must expect that civilization and political rights will oscillate between alternate perils—the peril that comes from the white man when he places civilization, or sometimes his travesty of it, higher than the Negro's political rights, and the peril that comes from the black man when his political rights are placed by himself or others higher than civilization—President James C. Willing, on "Race Education" in *The North American Review*, April, 1883.

out of its necessities, made them strong and permanent, society failed to impose such conditions as wise policy should have dictated, and now suffers the calamitous consequences. The tail wags the dog, instead of the dog wagging the tail.

No government can afford, with any degree of safety, to make four million of citizens out of so many slaves. And when it is remembered that our slaves were turned loose upon their former masters—lifted by one stroke of the pen, as it were, from the most degraded condition to the very pinnacle of sovereign manhood—the equals in unrestricted manhood, with the privileges and immunities of citizens who had been born to rule, apparently, instead of being ruled—it will be seen readily how critical was the situation.

But the condition having once been created by the strong arm of the Federal Government, based upon a bloody and costly war in open defiance of the Constitution as designed by the compromising Fathers of the Republic; the slave once made a free man the same as his former master, and given the ballot, the highest privilege of government a man can exercise;—the Government having once gone so far, there was absolutely nothing for it to do but to interpose its omnipotent authority between the haughty and arrogant free man on the one hand and the crouching and fearful freed man on the other—the lion and the lamb. To do less would be more than cruel, it would be murderous;— the agency which created the condition was bound by all law and precedent to see that those conditions were maintained in their entirety. It could not evade the issue except at the expense of dignity, consistency and humanity. There was but one honorable course to pursue. Any other would be a horrible abandonment of principle. If it were powerful to create, to make free men and citizens, it must, manifestly, be powerful to insure the enjoyment of the freedom conferred, and protect the inviolability of the franchise granted. Any other conclusion would make government a by-word and a scoffing to the nations; any other conclusion would make its conferring of freedom and citizenship absurd in the extreme, a mere trick of the demagogue to ease the popular conscience. To do such a thing would sink a decent government lower in the estimation of the world than the miserable apology of government represented by the Khedive of Egypt.

No patriotic American would admit to himself, or to a foreigner, that the United States Government, through its accredited representatives in Congress, possessed constitutional power to confer a benefit and did not possess power to make that benefit available; to contract an obligation, pecuniary or other, which it had not inherent power to liquidate. The validity of a contract, as a matter of fact, depends upon the ability of the parties to enter into it, for no court can enforce a contract when it is shown that the principals to it had not legal right to make it or to fulfill the conditions of it. It is accepted as a surety of power to observe the conditions when a sovereign government makes itself a party to a contract. The people are bound by their agents, to whom they delegate authority. Nothing is regarded in a more obnoxious light than the repudiation of their honest debts by sovereign States. It is regarded in financial circles as the crime of all crimes the blackest. The credit of the State is reduced to a song, and moneyed men shun it as they would a rattlesnake. The State and its people are held up as monsters of depravity. It matters not how unjust the debt, how poor the people; the mere fact that they repudiate an obligation which they entered into in good faith is sufficient to destroy their credit in New York or London and make them the target of every virtuous newspaper which voices the sentiment of the class that deals in "futures" and "corners." As an illustration, take the State of Virginia. The people of that State contracted large debts to aid and abet the cause of the so-called Confederate Government, a thing which crystallized around the question: "Have the Sovereign States absolute, undivided authority to regulate their own internal concerns, slave and other, or is this authority vested in the Federal or National Government?" When the people of Virginia contracted those large debts, drawing upon her future resources, and placing burdens upon men yet unborn, to propagate theories at variance with sound doctrines of government, and to perpetuate an institution too vile to be mentioned with respect, in 1860, and immediately subsequent thereto, when the State of Virginia contracted the debts in question for the perpetuation of slavery, she had a population of 1,047,299; 65.6 per cent of which was white (free), and 34.4 per cent was colored (slave). Virginia, therefore, in contracting debts in 1860, did not calculate that twenty-two years thereafter the obligations would be repudiated, and the credit of the State depreciated, by the assistance of the very class of persons to bind whom to a cruel and barbarous servitude those debts were contracted. It is one of the most striking instances of retributive justice that I ever knew. Nothing was more natural, when the question came up for final settlement a few years ago, than that the black voters of Virginia should take sides with those who opposed the full settlement of the indebtedness. It is too much to expect of sensible men that they will assent, in a state of sovereign citizenship, to cancel debts contracted when they had no voice in the matter, and when, as a matter of fact, the debts were contracted to rivet upon them the chains of death. And yet for the part the black men of Virginia took upon the settlement of her infamous debt, they have been abused and maligned from one end of the country to the other. Because they refused to vote to tax themselves to pay money borrowed without their consent, and applied to purposes of death and slaughter, no man has been found to commend them or to accept as sufficiently extenuating, the peculiar circumstances surrounding the question. Shylock must have his pound of flesh, though the unlucky victim bleed his life away. But there are laws "higher" than any framed in the interest of tyrannical capital. In my opinion, the man who deliberately invests his money to perpetuate so vile an institution as slavery deserves not only to lose the interest upon his investment but the principal as well. I therefore have not a grain of sympathy for the greedy cormorants who invested their money in the so-called Confederate Government. Neither have I any sympathy for the people of the South who, having invested all their money in human flesh, found themselves at the close of the Rebellion paupers in more senses than one—being bankrupt in purse and unused to make an honest living by honest labor—too proud to work and too poor to loaf.

In a question of this kind, no one disputes the power of Virginia to contract debts to propagate opinions, erroneous or other, but it is a question whether the people of one generation have the right to tax—that is, enslave—the people of generations yet unborn. The creation of public debts is pernicious in practice, productive of more harm than good. What right have I to create debts for my grandson or granddaughter? I have no right even to presume that I will have a grandson, certainly none that he will be able to meet his own debts in addition to those I entail upon him. The character of the people called upon to settle the debt of Virginia, contracted in 1860, before or immediately after, differed radically from the character of the people who were called upon to tax themselves to cancel that debt. Not only had the character of the people undergone a radical change; the whole social and industrial mechanism of the state had undergone a wonderful, almost an unrecognizable, metamorphosis. The haughty aristocrat, with his magnificent plantation, his army of slaves, and his "cattle on a thousand hills," who eagerly contracted the debt, had been transformed into a sour pauper when called upon to honor his note; while the magnificent plantation had been in many instances cut into a thousand bits to make homes for the former slaves, now freemen and citizens, the equals of "my lord," while "his cattle on a thousand hills" had dwindled down to a stubborn jackass and a worn out milch cow. True, the white man possessed, largely, the soil; but he was, immediately after the war, utterly incapable of wringing from it the bounty of Nature; he had first to be re-educated.

But, when the bloody rebellion was over, the country, in its sovereign capacity, and by individual States, was called upon to deal with grave questions growing out of the conflict. Mr. Lincoln, by a stroke of the pen,* transferred the battle from the field to the halls of legislation. In view of the "Emancipation proclamation "as issued by Mr. Lincoln, and the invaluable service rendered by black troops† in the rebellion, legislation upon the status of the former slave could not be avoided. The issue could not be evaded; like Banquo's ghost, it would not down. There were not wanting men, even when the war had ended and the question of chattel slavery had been forever relegated to the limbo of "things that were," who were willing still to toy with half-way measures, to cater to the caprices of that treacherous yet brave power—the South. They had not yet learned that Southern sentiment was fundamentally revolutionary, dynamic in the extreme, and could not be toyed with as with a doll-baby. So the statesmen proceeded to manufacture the "Reconstruction policy"—a policy more fatuous, more replete with fatal concessions and far more fatal omis-

---

* By virtue of the power and for the purposes aforesaid, I do ordain and declare that all persons held as slaves within said designated States and parts of States, are and henceforth shall be free; and that the Executive Government of the United States, including the military and naval authorities thereof, will recognize and maintain the freedom of said persons.—Abraham Lincoln's *Emancipation Proclamation.*

† From Williams's *History of the Negro Race in America* I construct the following table showing the number of colored troops employed by the Federal Government during the war of the Rebellion:

	Colored Troops Furnished 1861-65
Total of New England States	7,916
Total of Middle States	13,922
Total, Western States and Territories	12,711
Total, Border States	45,184
Total, Southern States	63,571
Grand Total States	143,304
At Large	733
Not accounted for	5,083
Officers	7,122
Grand total	156,242

This gives colored troops enlisted in the States in Rebellion; besides this, there were 92,576 colored troops (included with the white soldiers) in the quotas of the several States.

sions than any ever before adopted for the acceptance and governance of a rebellious people on the one hand and a newly made, supremely helpless people on the other. It is not easy to regard with equanimity the blunders of the "Reconstruction policy" and the manifold infamies which have followed fast upon its adoption.

The South scornfully rejected and successfully nullified the legislative will of the victors.

Judge Albion W. Tourgee says of this policy in his book called *A Fool's Errand:* "It was a magnificent sentiment that underlay it all,—an unfaltering determination, an invincible defiance to all that had the seeming of compulsion or tyranny. One cannot but regard with pride and sympathy the indomitable men, who, being conquered in war, yet resisted every effort of the conqueror to change their laws, their customs, or even the *personnel* of their ruling class; and this, too, not only with unyielding stubbornness, but with success. One cannot but admire the arrogant boldness with which they charged the nation which had overpowered them —even in the teeth of her legislators—with perfidy, malice, and a spirit of unworthy and contemptible revenge. How they laugred to scorn the Reconstruction Acts of which the wise men boasted! How boldly they declared the conflict to be irrepressible, and that white and black could not and should not live together as co-ordinate ruling elements! How lightly they told the tales of blood— of the Masked Night-Riders, of the Invisible Empire of Rifle clubs and Saber clubs (all organized for peaceful purposes), of warnings and whippings and slaughter! Ah, it is wonderful! * * * Bloody as the reign of Mary, barbarous as the chronicles of the Comanche!"

CHAPTER V

Illiteracy—Its Causes

At the close of the rebellion there were in the Union (according to the census of 1860) 4,441,830 people of African origin; in 1880 they had increased to 6,580,793. Of this vast multitude in 1860, it is safe to say, not so many as one in every ten thousand could read or write. They had been doomed by the most stringent laws to a long night of mental darkness. It was a crime to teach a black man how to read even the Bible, the sacred repository of the laws that must light the pathway of man from death unto life eternal. For to teach a slave was to make a firebrand—to arouse that love of freedom which stops at nothing short of absolute freedom. It is not, therefore, surprising that every southern state should have passed the most odious inhibitary laws, with severe fines and penalties for their infraction, upon the question of informing the stunted intelligence of the slave population. The following table [on p. 29] will show the condition of education in the South in 1880.

Speaking in the Senate of the United States June 13, 1882, the bill for National "Aid to Common Schools" being under consideration, Senator Henry W. Blair, of New Hampshire, said:

Excluding the states of Maryland and Missouri and the District of Columbia, and the total yearly expenditure for both races is only $7,339,932, while in the whole country the annual expenditure is, from taxation, $70,341,435, and from school funds $6,580,632, or a total of $76,922,067, (see tables 2 and 7,) or one-tenth of the whole, while they contain one-fifth of the school-population. The causes which have produced this state of things in the Southern States are far less important than the facts themselves as they now exist. To

COMPARATIVE STATISTICS OF EDUCATION AT THE SOUTH

States	White			Colored			Total expenditure for both races[a]
	School population	Enrollment	Percentage of the school population enrolled	School population	Enrollment	Percentage of the school population enrolled	
Alabama	217,590	107,483	49	170,413	72,007	42	$375,465
Arkansas	[b]181,799	[c]53,229	29	[b]54,332	[c]17,743	33	238,056
Delaware	31,505	25,053	80	3,954	2,770	70	207,281
Florida	[b]46,410	[c]18,871	41	[b]42,099	[c]20,444	49	114,895
Georgia	[d]236,319	150,134	64	[d]197,125	86,399	45	471,029
Kentucky	[e]478,597	[c]241,679	50	[e]66,564	[c]23,902	36	803,490
Louisiana	[c]139,661	[d]44,052	32	[c]134,184	[d]34,476	26	480,320
Maryland	[f]213,669	134,210	63	[f]63,591	28,221	44	1,544,367
Mississippi	175,251	112,994	64	251,438	123,710	49	850,704
Missouri	681,995	454,218	67	41,489	22,158	53	3,152,178
N. Carolina	291,770	136,481	47	167,554	89,125	53	352,882
S. Carolina	[g]83,813	61,219	73	[g]144,315	72,853	50	324,629
Tennessee	403,353	229,290	57	141,509	60,851	43	724,862
Texas	[h]171,426	138,912	81	[h]62,015	47,874	77	753,346
Virginia	314,827	152,136	48	240,980	68,600	28	946,109
W. Virginia	202,364	138,799	68	7,749	4,071	53	716,864
District of Columbia	29,612	16,934	57	13,946	9,505	68	438,567
Total	3,899,961	2,215,674		1,803,257	784,709		12,475,044

[a] In Delaware the colored public schools have been supported by the school tax collected from colored citizens only; recently, however, they have received an appropriation of $2,400 from the State; in Kentucky the school-tax collected from colored citizens is the only State appropriation for the support of colored schools; in Maryland there is a biennial appropriation by the Legislature; in the District of Columbia one-third of the school moneys is set apart for colored public schools, and in the other States mentioned above the school moneys are divided in proportion to the school population without regard to race.

[b] Several counties failed to make race distinctions.

[c] Estimated.

[d] In 1879.

[e] For whites the school age is 6 to 20, for colored 6 to 16.

[f] Census of 1870.

[g] In 1877.

[h] These numbers include some duplicates; the actual school population is 230,527.

find a remedy and apply it is the only duty which devolves upon us. Without universal education, not only will the late war prove to be a failure, but the abolition of slavery be proved to be a tremendous disaster, if not a crime.

The country was held together by the strong and bloody embrace of war, but that which the nation might and did do to retain the integrity of its territory and of its laws by the expenditure of brute force will all be lost if, for the subjection of seven millions of men, by the statutes of the States is to be substituted the thraldom of ignorance and the tyranny of an irresponsible suffrage. Secession, and a confederacy founded upon slavery as its chief cornerstone, would be better than the future of the Southern States—better for both races, too—if the nation is to permit one-third, and that the fairest portion of its domain, to become the spawning ground of ignorance, vice, anarchy, and of every crime. The nation as such abolished slavery as a legal institution; but ignorance is slavery, and no matter what is written in your constitutions and your laws, slavery will continue until intelligence, handmaid of liberty, shall have illuminated the whole land with the light of her smile.

Before the war the Southern States were aristocracies, highly educated, and disciplined in the science of polities. Hence they preserved order and flourished at home, while they imposed their will upon the nation at large. Now all is changed. The suffrage is universal, and that means universal ruin unless the capacity to use it intelligently is created by universal education. Until the republican constitutions, framed in accordance with the Congressional reconstruction which supplanted the governments initiated by President Johnson, common-school systems, like universal suffrage, were unknown. Hence in a special manner the nation is responsible for the existence and support of those systems as well as for the order of things which made them necessary. That remarkable progress has been made under their influence is true, and that the common school is fast becoming as dear to the masses of the people at the South as elsewhere is also evident.

The Nation, through the Freedmen's Bureau, and perhaps to a limited extent in other ways, has expended five millions of dollars for the education of negroes and refugees in the earlier days of reconstruction, while religious charities have founded many special schools which have thus far cost some ten millions more. The Peabody fund has distilled the dews of heaven all over the South; but heavy rains are needed; without them every green thing must wither away.

This work belongs to the Nation. It is a part of the war. We have the Southern people as patriotic allies now. We are one; so shall we be forever. But both North and South have a fiercer and more doubtful fight with the forces of ignorance than they waged with each other during the bloody years which chastened the opening life of this generation.

The South lost in the destruction of property about two billion dollars and in prosecuting the war two billion more. No people can lose so much without seriously disarranging the entire mechanism of their government. It is for this reason, therefore, that the measure of "National Aid to Education" has so many and so persistent advocates. I wish to place myself among them. If the safety of republican government abides in the intelligence and virtue of the people, it can very readily be seen how much safety there is in the South at present. If it be true that an ulcer will vitiate the entire body, and endanger the life of the patient, we can see very plainly to what possible danger the spread of illiteracy may lead us.

Illiteracy in the South is one of the worst legacies which the rebellion bequeathed to the nation. It has been the prime cause of more misgovernment in the South than any other one cause, not even the insatiable repacity of the carpet-bag adventurers taking precedence of it. It has not only served as a provocation to peculation and chicanery, but it has nerved the courage of the assassin and made merry the midnight ride of armed mobs bent upon righting wrongs by committing crimes before which the atrocities of savage warfare pale. Wholesale murders have been committed and sovereign majorities awed into silence and inaction by reason of the widespread illiteracy of the masses. The very first principles of republican government have been ruthlessly trampled under foot because the people were ignorant of their sovereign rights, and had not, therefore, courage to maintain them.

That there should be in sixteen States and the District of Columbia a population of 5,703,218 people to be educated out of $12,475,044 is sufficient to arouse the apprehension of the most indifferent friend of good government. The State of New York alone, with a school population of only 1,641,173 spent, in 1880, $9,675,922.

But I base my argument for the establishment and maintenance of a comprehensive system of National education upon other grounds than the "safety of the Union," which is the same argument used by Mr. Lincoln when he emancipated the slaves. This argument is strong, and will always greatly influence a certain class of people. And, naturally, it should, for the perpetuation of the Union is simply the perpetuation of a republican form of government. But there are stronger grounds to be considered.

1. The United States government is directly responsible for the illiteracy and the widespread poverty which obtain in the South. Under its sanction and by its connivance the institution of slavery flourished and prospered, until it had taken such deep root as to be almost impossible of extirpation. It was the *Union*, and not the *States*, severally, which made slavery part and parcel of the fundamental law of the land. If this be a correct statement of the case, and I assume that it is, the *Union* (and not the *States*, severally) is responsible for the ignorance of the black people of the South. Slavery could not have existed and grown in the Union save by permission of all the States of the Union. It is therefore obvious that the agency which created and fostered a great crime is obligated, not only by the laws of God but of man as well, to assume the responsibility of its creation and to remedy, as far as possible, the evil results of that crime. The issue cannot be evaded. The obligation rests upon the Union, not upon the several States, to assume the direction of methods by which the appalling illiteracy of the South is to be diminished.

2. There have not been wanting men and newspapers to urge that the United States should reimburse the slave-holders of the South for the wholesale confiscation, so to speak, of their property. True, these men and newspapers belong to that class of un-repentants who believed that slavery was a *Divine institution* and that the slave-holder was a sort of vicegerent of heaven, a holy Moses, as it were. But when we leave the absurdity of this claim, which lies upon the surface, there is much apparent reason in their representations. It was the *Union* which legalized the sale and purchase of slave property, thereby inviting capitalists to

invest in it; and it was the *Union* which declared such contracts null and void by the abolition of slavery, or confiscation of slave property. As I said before, I have no sympathy with those who invested their money in slave property. They not only received their just deserts in having their property confiscated, but they should have been compelled to make restitution to the last penny to the poor slaves whom they had systematically robbed. But perhaps this would have been carrying justice too near the ideal. For the great debt to the slave, who was robbed of his honest wage, we go behind the slave-holder, who had been invited by the government to invest his money in blood; we go to the head of the firm for the payment of debts contracted by the firm, for each member of the government is, measurably, an agent of the government, contracting and paying debts by its delegated authority. Thus the law holds him guilty who willfully breaks a contract entered into in good faith by all the parties to it. Instead of holding the slave-holder responsible for the robbery of the black man through a period of a hundred years, we hold the *government* responsible.

What man can compute the dollars stolen from the black slave in the shape of wages, for a period of a hundred years! What claim has the slave-holder against the government for confiscation of property by the side of the claim of the slaves for a hundred years of wages and enervated and dwarfed manhood! A billion dollars would have bought every slave in the South in 1860, but fifty billions would not have adequately recompensed the slave for enforced labor and debased manhood. The debt grows in magnitude the closer it is inspected. And yet there are those who will laugh this claim to scorn; who will be unable to see any grounds upon which to base the justice of it; who will say that the black man was fully compensated for all the ills he had borne, the robbery to which he had been subjected, and the debasement—not to say enervation—of his manhood, by the great act by which he was made a free man and a citizen.

But there is, or should be, such a claim; it rests upon the strong-est possible grounds of equity; while the conference of freedom and citizenship was simply the rendering back in the first instance that which no man has any right to appropriate, law or no law; and, in the second, bestowing a boon which had been honestly earned in every conflict waged by the Union from Yorktown to Appomatox Court House—a boon, I am forced to exclaim, which has, in many respects, proved to be more of a curse than a bless-ing, more a dead weight to carry than a help to conserve his free-dom and to aid in the fixing of his proper status as a co-equal citizen. I deny the *right* of any man to enslave his fellow; I deny the *right* of any government, sovereign as the Union or dependent as are the States in many respects, to pass any regulation which robs *one man or class* to enrich *another*. Individuals may invest their capital in human flesh, and governments may legalize the infamous compact; yet it carries upon its face the rankest injus-tice to the man and outrage upon the laws of God, the common Parent of all mankind. There are those in this country—men too of large influence, however small their wit, who, aping miser-ably the masterly irony of *Junius*, speak of the black man as the "ward of the nation"—a sort of pauper, dependent upon the char-ity of a generous and humane people for sustenance, and even tolerance to dwell among them, to enjoy the blessing of a civiliza-tion which I pronounce to be reared upon quicksand, a civiliza-tion more fruitful of poverty, misery and crime than of com-petence, happiness and virtue. Those who regard the black man in the light of a "ward of the nation," are too narrow-minded, ignorant or ungenerous to deserve my contempt. The people of this country have been made fabulously affluent by legalized rob-bery of the black man; the coffers of the National Government have overflowed into the channels of subsidy and peculation, en-riching sharpers and thieves, with the earnings of slave labor; while nineteen out of every twenty landowners in the South ob-tained their unjust hold upon the soil by robbing the black man.

When the rebellion at last closed, the white people of the South were poor in gold but rich indeed in lands, while the black man was poor in everything, even in manhood, not because of any neglect or improvidence on his part, but because, though he labored from the rising to the setting of the sun, he received absolutely nothing for his labor, often being denied adequate food to sustain his physical man and clothing to protect him from the rude inclemency of the weather. He was a bankrupt in purse because the *government* had robbed him; he was a bankrupt in character, in all the elements of a successful manhood, because the *government* had placed a premium upon illiteracy and immorality. It was not the individual slave-owner who held the black man in chains; it was the *government;* for, the government having permitted slavery to exist, the institution vanished the instant the government declared that it should no longer exist!

I therefore maintain that the people of this Nation who enslaved the black man, who robbed him of more than a hundred years of toil, who perverted his moral nature, and all but extinguished in him the Divine spark of intelligence, are morally bound to do all that is in their power to build up his shattered manhood, to put him on his feet, as it were, to fit him to enjoy the freedom thrust upon him so unceremoniously, and to exercise with loyalty and patriotism the ballot placed in his hands—the ballot, in which is wrapped up the destiny of republican government, the perpetuity of democratic institutions. It is the proper function of government to see to it that its citizens are properly prepared to exercise wisely the liberties placed in their keeping. Self-preservation would dictate as much; for, if it be considered the better part of valor to discretely build and maintain arsenals and forts to bar out the invader, to prepare against the assaults of the enemy from without, how much more imperative it is to take timely precautions to counteract the mischief of insidious foes from within? Are our liberties placed more in jeopardy by the assaults of an enemy who plans our destruction three thousand miles away than of the enemy within our very bosoms? Was it the puissance of the barbarian arms or the corruption and enervation of the character of her people which worked the downfall of Rome? Was it influences from *without* or influences from *within* which corrupted the integrity of the people of Sparta and led to their subjugation by a more sturdy people? Let us learn by the striking examples of history. A people's greatness should be measured, not by its magnificent palaces, decked out in all the gaudy splendors of art and needless luxuries, the price of piracy or direct thievery; not in the number of colossal fortunes accumulated out of the stipend of the orphan and widow and the son of toil; not in the extent and richness of its public buildings and palaces of idle amusement; not in vast aggregations of capital in the coffers of the common treasury—capital unnecessarily diverted from the channels of trade, extorted from the people by the ignorance of their "wise men," who seek in vain for a remedy for the evil, *because they do not want to find one.** A people's greatness should not be measured by these standards, for they are the parasites which eat away the foundations of greatness and stability. On the contrary, such greatness is to be found in the general diffusion of wealth, the comparative contentment and competency of the masses, and the general virtue and patriotism of the *whole* people. It should, therefore, manifestly be the end and aim of legislators to so shape the machinery placed in their hands as to operate with the least possible restraint upon the energies of the people. It should not be the studied purpose to enrich the few at the expense of the many, to restrain this man and give that one the largest possible immunity. No law should be made or enforced which would abridge my right while enlarging the right of my neighbor. That such is the case at this time—that legislatures are manipulated in the interest of a few, and that the great mass of the people feel only the burdens placed upon them by their ser-

* Since all sensible men know that the evil lies in a protective tariff and the bulky catalogue of monopoly.

vants, who are more properly speaking become their masters— that to such perversion of popular sovereignty we have come, is admitted by candid men.

Therefore, that the people may more clearly know their rights and how best to preserve them and reap their fullest benefits, they should be instructed in the language which is the medium through which to interpret their grand *Magna Charta*.

CHAPTER VI

Education—Professional or Industrial

❖————◄◖∿☺➤◗►————❖

The "Religious Training of the Freedmen" and the "Education of the Freedmen" have raised up an army of people more *peculiar* in many respects than any other like class in all the history of mankind. They stand off by themselves; they are not to be approached by any counter method of "advocating a cause" or "building up the Kingdom of Christ" in *their* field. Millions of dollars have been "raised" to root out the illiteracy and immorality of the Freedmen, and to build up their shattered manhood. Indeed, there have been times when I have seriously debated the question, whether the black man had any manhood left, after the missionaries and religious enthusiasts had done picturing, or, rather, caricaturing his debased moral and mental condition. He has been made the victim of the most exalted panegyric by one set of fanatics, and of the most painful, malignant abuse and detraction by another set. The one has painted him as a sort of angel, and the other as a sort of devil; when, in fact, he is neither one nor the other; when, simply, he is a *man*, a member of the common family, possessing no more virtue nor vice than his brother, the brother who has managed to so impose upon himself that he is pretty thoroughly convinced that nature expended all its most choice materials in the construction of his class. But this is simply the work of the devil, who delights in throwing cayenne pepper into the eyes of good men.

The aspects of the work which has been done in the South for the colored people by "missionaries," so to term them, by the assistance of large sums of money donated by philanthropic men and women, are very many-sided indeed. I would in no wise underrate the magnitude of the work performed, nor attribute to those who have been the agents in disbursing these unparalleled benefactions motives other than of the purest and loftiest, in a majority of cases; but I think the time has arrived when we may disrobe the matter of the romance which writers have industriously woven about it. In the early stages of the work a few men and women of large fortunes, who had been "born with a silver spoon in their mouths," may have gone South to labor for humanity and the Master, may have left comfortable firesides and congenial companionships to make their homes among strangers who shut them out from their affections and sympathies because they had come to labor for the poor and the despised. Examples of this lofty devotion to a good cause there undoubtedly were in the days long ago; but the bulk of the work was performed by persons, male and female, to whom employment, an opportunity to make an honest living in an honest way, was a godsend. That they possessed much bravery to undertake a work which shut them out from the sympathy and social recognition of those who may be called their equals, is not denied; but that they were the pampered children of fortune, laboring simply for God and humanity, which zealous persons have painted them to be in newspapers and magazines, religious and other, is simply making a mountain out of a mole-hill. They were neither millionaires nor paupers, but they were educated men and women, like thousands throughout the North and West, who went into the field to labor because it was rich unto the harvest and the laborers were few. To say that salaries offered were not accepted always with promptness would be to get on the wrong side of a correct statement of fact. There are hundreds and thousands of educated men and women in the North and West to-day "waiting for something to turn up," and who would not hesitate a moment to embrace an

schools is obvious, and is sufficiently absurd to repel the sympathy or practical philanthropy of any man, Christian or Infidel. Why should the people be called upon to support *two* schools within speaking distance of each other to preserve an infamous distinction, a sneaking caste prejudice? Why! Because the people are wise in their own conceit—perfectly rational upon all other questions save the *color question*. The South is weighted down with debt, almost as poor as the proverbial "Job's turkey," and yet she supports a dual school system simple to gratify a *prejudice*. I notice with surprise that among the bills pending before Congress to give national aid to education it is not proposed to interfere with the irregular and ruinous dual caste schools; thereby, in effect, giving the national assent to a system repugnant to the genius of the constitution. But it is nothing new under the sun for the Congress of the Nation to aid and abet institutions and theories anti-republican and pernicious in all their ramifications.

Perhaps no people ever had more advantages to dedicate and prepare themselves for the ministry of Christ than the colored people of the South. The religious "idea" has been so thoroughly worked that other branches of study, other callings than the ministry, have paled into insignificance. The Cross of Christ has been held up before the colored youth as if the whole end and aim of life was to preach the Gospel, as if the philosophy of heaven superseded in practical importance the philosophy of life. The persistence with which this one "idea" has been forced upon colored students has produced the reverse of what was anticipated in a large number of cases, and very naturally. It is a false theory to suppose all the people of any one class to be specially fitted for only one branch of industry: for I maintain that preaching has largely become a trade or profession, in which the churches with large salaries have become prizes to be contended for with almost as much zeal and partisanship as the prizes in politics. This is true not only of colored ministers but white ones as well. It is no disparagement of colored ministers to say that day by day they grow more and more in favor of serving churches with fair salaries than in carrying around the cross as itinerants, without any special place to lay their heads when the storms blow and the rains descend. In this they do but pattern after white clergymen, who do not always set examples that angels would be justified in imitating.

Colored people are naturally sociable, and intensely religious in their disposition. Their excellent social qualities make them the best of companions. They are musical, humorous and generous to a fault. Coupled with their strong religious bias, these attractive qualities will in time lift them to the highest possible grade in our dwarfed civilization, where the fittest does not always survive; the drossiest, flimsiest, most selfish and superficial often occupying the high places, social and political. But I have still higher aspirations for my race. There is hope for any people who are social in disposition, for this supposes the largest capacity for mutual friendships, therefore of co-operation, out of which the highest civilization is possible to be evolved; while a love of music and the possession of musical and humorous talent is, undeniably, indicative of genius and prospective culture and refinement of the most approved standard.

Indeed, the constant evolution of negro character is one of the most marked and encouraging social phenomena of the times; it constantly tends upwards, in moral, mental development and material betterment. Those who contend that the negro is standing still, or *"relapsing into barbarism,"* are the falsest of false prophets. They resolutely shut their eyes to facts all around them, and devote columns upon columns of newspaper, magazine and book argument—imaginary pictures—to the immorality, mental sterility and innate improvidence of this people; and they do this for various reasons, none of them honorable, many of them really disreputable. In dealing with this negro problem they always start off upon a false premise; their conclusions must, necessarily, be false. In the first place, disregarding the fact that the negroes of the South are nothing more nor less than the laboring class of the people, the same in many particulars as the English and Irish peasantry, they proceed to regard them as intruders in the community—as a people who continually take from but add nothing to the wealth of the community.

It is nothing unusual to see newspaper articles stating in the most positive terms that the schools maintained by the State for the education of the blacks are supported out of the taxes paid by *white men;* and, very recently, it was spoken of as a most laudable act of justice and generosity that the State of Georgia paid out annually for the maintenance of colored schools more money than *the aggregate taxes paid into the treasury* of the State by the Negro property owners of the State; while the grand commonwealth of Kentucky only appropriates for the maintenance of colored schools such moneys as are paid into the State treasury by the colored people. Can the philosophy of taxation be reduced to a more hurtful, a more demoralizing absurdity!

Suppose the same standard of distribution of school funds should be applied to the city or the State of New York; what would be the logical result? Should we appropriate annually from nine to twelve millions of dollars to improve the morals of the people by informing their intelligence? Would the State be able, after ten years of such an experiment, to pay the myriads of officials which would be required to preserve the public peace, to protect life and insure proper respect for the so-called rights of property? Such an experiment would in time require the deportation to New York of the entire male adult population of Ireland, to be turned into the "finest police in the world," to stem the tide of crime and immorality which such premium upon ignorance would entail. Since even under the present munificent and well ordered school system, it is almost impossible to elect a Board of Aldermen from any other than the *slum* elements of the population—the liquor dealers, the gamblers, and men of their kind, the President of the New York Board of Aldermen at this very writing being a liquor-dealer, who can estimate the calamity which the inauguration of the Kentucky system would bring upon the people of New York—appropriating to the support of the public schools only such taxes as were paid by the parents of the children who attend them!

And, yet, there is hardly an editor in the South who does not regard it as so much robbery of the tax-payers to support schools for the colored people—for the proletarian classes generally, white and colored. They stoutly maintain that these people really add nothing to the stock of wealth, really produce nothing, and that, therefore charity can become no more magnanimous than when it gives, places in reach of, the poor man the opportunity to educate his child, the embryo man, the future citizen.

They think it a sounder principle of government to equip and maintain vast penal systems—with chain gangs, schools of crime, depravity and death, than to support schools and churches. Millions of money are squandered annually to curb crime, when a few thousand dollars, properly applied, would prove to be a more humane, a more profitable preventive. The poor school teacher is paid *twenty-five dollars per month* for three months in the year, while the prison guards is paid *fifty dollars per month* for twelve months—ninety days being the average length given to teach the child in the school and three hundred and sixty-five being necessary to teach him in the prison, whence he is frequently graduated a far worse, more hopeless enemy of society than when he matriculated.

And the brutality of the convict systems of Southern States is equaled by no similar institutions in the world, if we except the penal system enforced by Russia in Siberia. The terms of imprisonment for minor offenses are cruelly excessive, while the food and shelter furnished and the punishments inflicted would bring the blush of shame to the cheeks of a savage. The convict systems of Alabama, Georgia, South Carolina and Arkansas are a burning disgrace to the Christian civilization which we boast. Nothing short of a semi-barbarous public opinion would permit them to exist. Governors have "called attention" to them; legislatures have "investigated" and "resolved" that they should be purified, and a *few* newspapers here and there have held them up to the scorn and contempt of the world; yet they not only grow worse year by year, but the number of them steadily multiplies. And so they will. How is it to be otherwise? To prevent such ulcerations upon the body you must purify the blood. You cannot root them out by probing; that simply aggravates them.

A system of misrepresentation and vilification of the character and condition of the Southern Negro has grown up, for the avowed purpose of enlisting the sympathies of the charitable and philanthropic people of the country to supply funds for his regeneration and education, which the government, State and Federal, studiously denies; so that it is almost impossible to form a correct opinion either of his moral, mental or material condition. Societies have organized and maintain a work among that people which requires an annual outlay of millions of dollars and thousands of employees; and to maintain the work, to keep up the interest of the charitable, it is necessary to picture, as black as imagination can conceive it, the present and prospective condition of the people who are, primarily, the beneficiaries. The work and its maintenance has really become a heavy strain upon the patience and generosity of the liberal givers of the land—whose profuse behests have no parallel in the history of any people. They have kept it up wellnigh a quarter of a century; and it is no disparagement to their zeal to say the tax upon them is becoming more of a burden than a pleasure. They have done in the name of humanity and of God for the unfortunate needy what the government should have done for its own purification and perpetuity for the co-equal citizen. And it is high time that the government should relieve the individual from the unjust and onerous tax.

I do not hesitate to affirm, that while the work done by the charitable for the black citizen of this Republic has been of the most incalculable benefit to him, it has also done him injury which it will take years upon years to eradicate. The misrepresentations resorted to, to obtain money to "lift him up," have spread broadcast over the land a feeling of contempt for him as a man and pity for his lowly and unfortunate condition; so that throughout the North a business man would much rather *give a thousand dollars* to aid in the education of the black heathen than to give a black scholar and gentleman an opportunity to honestly *earn a hundred dollars.* He has no confidence in the capacity of the black man. He has seen him pictured a savage, sunk in ignorance and vice—an object worthy to receive alms, but incapable of making an honest living. So that when a black man demonstrates any capacity, shows any signs of originality or genius, rises just a few inches above the common, he at once becomes an object rare and wonderful—a "Moses," a *"leader* of his people."—It is almost as hard for an educated black man to obtain a position of trust and profit as it is for a camel to go through the eye of a needle. The missionaries, the preachers, and the educators, assisted by the newspapers and the magazines, have educated the people into the false opinion that it is safer to "donate" a thousand dollars to a colored college than it is to give one black man a chance to make an honest living.

Let us now look at the system of education as it has been operated among the colored people of the South.

It cannot be denied that much of the fabulous sums of money lavishly given for the education of the Freedmen of the South, has been squandered upon experiments, which common sense should have dictated were altogether impracticable. Perhaps this was sequential in the early stages of the work, when the instructor was ignorant of the topography of the country, the temper of the people among whom he was to labor, and, more important still, when he was totally ignorant of the particular class upon whom he was to operate—ignorant of their temperament, receptive capacity and peculiar, aye, unique, idiosyncrasies. Thus thousands upon thousands of dollars were expended upon the erection and endowment of "colleges" in many localities where ordinary common schools were unknown. Each college was, therefore, necessarily provided with a primary department, where the child of ten years and the adult of forty struggled in the same classes with the first elements of rudimentary education. The child and the adult each felt keenly his position in the college, and a course of cramming was pursued, injurious to all concerned, to lessen the number in the primary and to increase the number in the college departments. No man can estimate the injury thus inflicted upon not only the student but the cause of education. Even unto to-day there are colleges in localities in the South which run all year while the common school only runs from three to eight months.

Indeed, the multiplication of colleges and academies for the "higher education of colored youth" is one of the most striking phenomena of the times: as if theology and the classics were the things best suited to and most urgently needed by a class of persons unprepared in rudimentary education, and whose immediate aim must be that of the mechanic and the farmer—to whom the classics, theology and the sciences, in their extremely impecunious state, are unequivocable abstractions. There will be those who will denounce me for taking this view of collegiate and professional preparation; but I maintain that any education is false which is unsuited to the condition and the prospects of the student. To educate him for a lawyer when there are no clients, for medicine when the patients, although numerous, are too poor to give him a living income, to fill his head with Latin and Greek as a teacher when the people he is to teach are to be instructed in the *a b c's*—such education is a waste of time and a senseless expenditure of money.

I do not inveigh against higher education; I simply maintain that the sort of education the colored people of the South stand

most in need of is *elementary and industrial.* They should be instructed for the work to be done. Many a colored farmer boy or
mechanic has been spoiled to make a foppish gambler or loafer, a
swaggering pedagogue or a cranky homiletician. Men may be
spoiled by education, even as they are spoiled by illiteracy. Education is the preparation for a future work; hence men should be
educated with special reference to that work.

If left to themselves men usually select intuitively the course
of preparation best suited to their tastes and capacities. But the
colored youth of the South have been allured and seduced from
their natural inclination by the premiums placed upon theological, classical and professional training for the purpose of sustaining the reputation and continuance of "colleges" and their
professorships.

I do not hesitate to say that if the vast sums of money already
expended and now being spent in the equipment and maintenance
of colleges and universities for the so called "higher education"
of colored youth had been expended in the establishment and
maintenance of primary schools and schools of applied science,
the race would have profited vastly more than it has, both men-
tally and materially, while the results would have operated far
more advantageously to the State, and satisfactorily to the munificent benefactors.

Since writing the above, I find in a very recent number of
Judge Tourgèe's magazine, *The Continent,* the following reflec-
tions upon the subject, contributed to that excellent periodical by
Prof. George F. Magoun of Iowa College. Mr. Magoun says:

May I offer one suggestion which observation a few years since among the
freedmen and much reflection, with comparisons made in foreign countries,
have impressed upon me? It is this, that the key of the future for the black
men of the South is *industrial* education. The laboring men of other lands
cannot hold their own in skilled labor save as they receive such education,
and this of a constantly advancing type. The English House of Commons
moved two years since for a Royal Commission to study the technical schools
of the continent, and the report respecting France made by this commission

has been republished at Washington by the United States Commissioner of Education. In our two leading northwestern cities, St. Louis and Chicago, splendid manual training-schools have been formed, and east and west the question of elementary manual training in public schools is up for discussion and decision. All this for *white* laboring men. As long ago as December, 1879, the Legislature of Tennessee authorized a brief manual of the Elementary Principles of Agriculture to be "taught in the public schools of the State," for the benefit of *white* farmers again. The Professor of Chemistry in the Vanderbilt University, Nashville, prepared the book—107 pages. Where in all this is there anything for the educational improvement of the black laborer just where he needs education most? The labor of the South is subject in these years to a marvelous revolution. The only opportunity the freedman has to rise is by furnishing such skilled labor as the great changes going on in that splendid section of the land require. How can he furnish it, unless the education given him is chiefly industrial and technical? Some very pertinent statements of the situation are made in the *Princeton Review* for May. They confirm all that you have said.* As to the various bills before Congress, the writer says: "Immediate assistance should be rendered to the ex-slave States in the development of an education suited to their political and *industrial* needs." Can this be an education in Latin and Greek?" (The writer contends earnestly for retaining these studies in classical college and academy courses for students of all colors.) Can it be anything else than training in elementary industry, such as is now demanded for our Northern common-schools? If the denominational freedmen's schools find this a necessity, is it anything less for the Southern public schools act which is contemplated in the bills before Congress?

Mr. Magoun reasons wisely. If the colored men of the South are to continue their grip as the wage-workers and wealth-producers of that section they must bring to their employments common intelligence and skill; and these are to be obtained in the South as in the North, by apprenticeship and in schools specially provided for the purpose. Instead of spending three to seven years in mastering higher education, which presupposes favorable conditions, colored youth should spend those years in acquiring a "common school education," and in mastering some trade by which to make an honest livelihood when they step forth into the world of fierce competition.

* Judge Tourgee has for years been urgently and admirably writing in advocacy of National Aid in Southern Education.

Some may ask: Shall we, then, not have some scholars, men learned in all that higher education gives? Of course; and we should have them. Men fitted by nature for special pursuits in life will make preparation for that work. Water will find its level. Genius cannot be repressed. It will find an audience, even though the singer be Robert Burns at his plow in the remoteness of Ayr, or the philosophic Æsop in the humble garb of a Greek pedant's slave. Genius will take care of itself; it is the mass of mankind that must be led by the hand as we lead a small boy. It is therefore that I plead, that the masses of the colored race should receive such preparation for the fierce competition of every day life that the odds shall not be against them. I do not plead for the few, who will take care of themselves, but for the many who must be guided and protected lest they fall a prey to the more hardy or unscrupulous.

Mr. Magoun follows out his train of thought in the following logical deductions:

Plainly, if this opportunity for furnishing the skilled labor of the South hereafter (as he has furnished the unskilled heretofore) slips away from the black man, he can never rise. In the race for property, influence, and all success in life, the industrially educated white man—whatever may be said of Southern white men "hating to work"—will outstrip him. Before an ecclesiastical body of representative colored men at Memphis, in the autumn of 1880, I urged this consideration, when asked to advise them about education, as the one most germane to their interests; and preachers and laymen, and their white teachers, approved every word, and gave me most hearty thanks. I counseled aspiring young men to abstain from unsuitable attempts at merely literary training; from overlooking the intermediate links of culture in striving after something "beyond their measure;" from expecting any more to be shot up into the United States Senatorships, etc., by a revolution which had already wellnigh spent its first exceptional force (as a few extraordinary persons are thrown up into extraordinary distinction in the beginning of revolutions); from ambitious rejection of the steady, thorough, toilsome methods of fitting themselves for immediate practical duties and nearer spheres, by which alone any class is really and healthfully elevated. To shirk elementary preparation and aspire after the results of scholarship without its painstaking processes is THE *temptation of colored students*, as I know by having taught them daily in college classes. I rejoice in every such student who really climbs the heights of learning with exceeding joy. But a far greater proportion than has thus far submitted to thorough-going preparation for skilled labor must do so, or there is no great future for them in this land as a race.

But already the absurdity of beginning at the apex of the educational fabric instead of at the base is being perceived by those who have in hand the education of colored youth. A large number of colleges are adding industrial to their other features, and with much success, and a larger number of educators are agitating the wisdom of such feature.

Perhaps no educational institution in the Union has done more for the industrial education of the colored people of the South than the Hampton (Virginia) Normal and Agricultural Institute under the management of General S. C. Armstrong. The success of this one institution in industrial education, and the favor with which it is regarded by the public, augurs well for the future of such institutions. That they many multiply is the fervent wish of every man who apprehends the necessities of the colored people.

In a recent issue of the *New York Globe,* Prof. T. McCants Stewart of the Liberia (West Africa) College, who is studying the industrial features of the Hampton Normal and Agricultural Institute for use in his capacity as a professor among the people of the Lone Star Republic, photographs in the following manner the great work being done at Hampton. Prof. Stewart says:

> The day after my arrival, I was put into the hands of an excellent New England gentleman, who was to show me through the Institute. He took me first to the barn, a large and substantial building in which are stored the products of the farm, and in which the stock have their shelter. We ascended a winding staircase, reached the top, and looked down upon the Institute grounds with their wide shell-paved walls, grassplots, flower-beds, orchards, groves and many buildings—the whole full of life, and giving evidence of abundant prosperity, and surrounded by a beautiful and charming country. We came down and began our rounds through "the little world" in which almost every phase of human life has its existence.
>
> We went into the shoe-making department. It is in the upper part of a two-story brick building. On the first floor the harness-making department is located. We were told that Frederick Douglass has his harness made here. One

certainly gets good material and honest work; and reasonable prices are charged. In the shoe department several Indian boys and youths were at work. There were also three or four colored boys. They make annually for the United States government two thousand pairs of shoes for the Indians. They also look after outside orders, and do all the repairing, etc., of boots and shoes for the faculty, officers, and students—making fully five thousand pairs of shoes a year, if we include the repairing in this estimate. At the head of this department is a practical shoemaker from Boston. Each department has a practical man at its head. We visited, not all the first day, the blacksmith, wheelwright and tin shops, and looked through the printing office, and the knitting-room, in which young men are engaged manufacturing thousands of mittens annually for a firm in Boston. These two departments are in a commodious brick edifice, called the "Stone Building." It is the gift of Mrs. Valeria Stone.

One of the most interesting departments is located also in the "Stone Building"—the sewing-room. In it are nearly a score, perhaps more, of cheerful, busy girls. The rapid ticking of the machine is heard, and the merry laugh followed by gentle whispers gives life to the room. These young girls are the future wives and mothers; and the large majority of them will be married to poor men. In the kitchen, the laundry, and the sewing-room, they are acquiring a knowledge and habits of industry that will save their husbands' pennies, and thus keep them from living from hand to mouth, making an everlasting struggle to save their nose from the grindstone. In the schoolroom, they are gathering up those intellectual treasures, which will make them in a double sense helpmeets unto their husbands.

Standing in the carpenter and paint shops, and in the saw mill, and seeing Negro youths engaged in the most delicate kind of work, learning valuable and useful trades, I could not help from feeling that this is an excellent institution, and that I would like to have my boys spend three years here, from fourteen to seventeen, grow strong in the love for work, and educated to feel the dignity of labor, and get a trade: then if they have the capacity and desire to qualify for a "top round in the ladder," for leadership in the "world's broad field of battle," it will be time enough to think of Harvard and Yale and Edinburgh, or perhaps similar African institutions.

Mr. George H. Corliss, of Rhode Island, presented to the school in 1879 a sixty-horse power Corliss engine. Soon after Mr. C. P. Huntington, of the Missouri & Pacific R.R., gave a saw mill, and as a result of these gifts large industrial operations were begun. The saw mill is certainly an extensive enterprise. Logs are brought up from the Carolinas, and boards are sawn out, and in the turning department fancy fixtures are made for houses, piazzas, etc.

There are two farms. The Normal School farm, and the Hemenway farm, which is four miles from the Institute. On the former seventy tons of hay and about one hundred and twenty tons of ensilaged fodder-corn were raised last year, besides potatoes, corn, rye, oats, asparagus, and early vegetables. Five hundred thousand bricks were also made. The Hemenway farm, of five hundred acres, is in charge of a graduate and his wife. Its receipts reach nearly three thousand dollars a year, and the farm promises to do invaluable service in time towards sustaining this gigantic work. All of the industries do not pay. For example, the deficit in the printing office last year was about seven hundred dollars. This is due to the employment and training of student labor. The primary aim is not the making of money but the advancement of the student. After they learn, they are good, profitable workmen; but they then leave the Institute to engage in the outside world in the battle of life. On the farm is a large number of stock, milch cows and calves, beef cattle, horses and colts, mules, oxen, sheep and hogs—in all nearly five hundred heads.

In these various industries, the farm, saw mill, machine shop, knitting, carpentering, harness making, tinsmithing, blacksmithing, shoe-making, wheelwrighting, tailoring, sewing, printing, etc., over five hundred students were engaged in 1883. They earned over thirty thousand dollars—an average of seventy dollars each. There is no question about the fact that this is a "beehive" into which a bee can enter, if accepted, with nothing but his soul and his muscle, and get a good education!

Professor Stewart's article carries upon its face the proper reply to Mr. Magoun's apprehensions and my own deductions, and is the very strongest argument for a complete and immediate recasting of the underlying principles upon which nearly all colored colleges are sustained and operated.

Money contributed for eleemosynary purposes is a sacred trust, and should so be applied as to net the greatest good not only to the beneficiary but the donor. The primary object of educational effort among the colored people thus far has been to purify their perverted moral nature and to indoctrinate in them correcter ideas of religion and its obligations; and the effort has not been in vain. Yet I am constrained to say, the inculcation of these principals has been altogether a too predominant idea. Material possibilities are rightly predicated upon correct moral and spiritual bases; but a morally and spiritually sound training must be sustained by such preparation for the actual work of life, as we find it in the machine shop, the grain field, and the commercial pursuits. The moralist and missionary are no equals for the man

whose ideas of honest toil are supplemented by a common school
training and an educated hand. This is exemplified every day in
the ready demand for foreign-born skilled labor over our own
people, usually educated as gentlemen without means, as if they
were to be kid-gloved fellows, not men who must contend for subsistence with the horny-handed men who have graduated from the
machine shops and factories and the schools of applied sciences
of Europe. Indeed, the absence of the old-time apprentices among
the white youth of the North, as a force in our industrial organization to draw upon, can be accounted for upon no other ground
than that the supply of foreign-born skilled help so readily fills
the demand that employers find it a useless expenditure of means
to graduate the American boy. Thus may we account for the
"grand rush" young men make for the lighter employments and
the professions, creating year after year an idle floating population of miseducated men, and reducing the compensation for
clerical work below that received by hod-carriers. This is not a
fancy picture; it is an arraignment of the American system of education, which proceeds upon the assumption that boys are all
"born with a silver spoon in their mouths" and are destined to
reach—not the poor-house, but the Senate House or the White
House.

The American system of education proceeds upon a false and
pernicious assumption; and, while I protest against its application generally, I protest, in this connection, against its application in the case of the colored youth in particular. What the
colored boy, what all boys of the country need, is *industrial not
ornamental* education; shall they have it? Let the State and the
philanthropists answer.

feel that justice will prevail. Progress goes forward ever, backward never.

That human intelligence has reached higher ground within the present century than it ever before attained, goes without saying. That we have marvelously improved upon all the mechanism of government is equally true. But whether we have improved upon the time-honored rules of dealing with rebels by extending to them general amnesty for all their sins of commission is seriously to be debated. If we may judge of the proper treatment of treason by the example which, according to Milton, High Heaven made of Lucifer, amnesty is a failure; if we may judge by the almost absolute failure of the results of the war of the Rebellion, we may emphatically pronounce amnesty to be a noxious weed which should not be permitted to take too firm a rooting in our dealing with traitors. Human, it may be, to err, and to forgive Divine; but for man to extend forgiveness too far is positively fatal. Examples are not wanting to show the truthfulness of the reasoning.

There is no error which has been productive of more disaster and death than the stupid plan adopted by the Federal government in what is known as the "Reconstruction policy." This *policy*, born out of expediency and nurtured in selfishness, was, in its inception, instinct with the elements of failure and of death. Perhaps no piece of legislation, no policy, was ever more fatuous in every detail. How could it be otherwise? How could the men who devised it expect for it anything more than a speedy, ignominious collapse? All the past history of the Southern states unmistakably pointed to the utter failure of any policy in which the whites were not made the masters; unless, indeed, they were subjected to that severe governmental control which their treason merited, until such time as the people were prepared for self-government by education, the oblivion of issues out of which the war grew, the passing away by death of the old spirits, and the complete metamorphosis of the peculiar conditions predicated upon and fostered by the unnatural state of slavery.

At the close of the Rebellion, in 1865, the United States government completely transformed the social fabric of the Southern state governments; and, without resorting to the slow process of educating the people; without even preparing them by proper warnings; without taking into consideration the peculiar relations of the subject and dominant classes—the slave class and the master class—instantly, as it were, the lamb and the lion were commanded to lie down together. The master class, fresh from the fields of a bloody war, with his musket strapped to his shoulder and the sharp thorn of ignominious defeat penetrating his breast; the master class, educated for two hundred years to dominate in his home, in the councils of municipal, state and Federal government; the master class, who had been taught that slavery was a divine institution and that the black man, the unfortunate progeny of Ham, was his lawful slave and property; and the slave class, born to a state of slavery and obedience, educated in the school of improvidence, mendacity and the lowest vices—these two classes of people, born to such widely dissimilar stations in life and educated in the most extreme schools, were declared to be *free, and equal before the law,* with the right to vote; to testify in courts of law; to sit upon jury and in the halls of legislation, municipal and other; to sue and be sued; to buy and to sell; to marry and give in marriage. In short, these two classes of people were made co-equal citizens, entitled alike to the protection of the laws and the benefits of government.

I know of no instance in the various history of mankind which equals in absurdity the presumption of the originators of our "Reconstruction policy" that the master class would accept cordially the conditions forced upon them, or that the enfranchised class would prove equal to the burden so unceremoniously forced upon them. On the one hand, a proud and haughty people, who had stubbornly contested the right of the government to interfere with the extension of slavery, not to say confiscation of slave property —a people rich in lands, in mental resources, in courage; on the other, a poor, despised people, without lands, without money, without mental resources, without moral character—these peoples *equal*, indeed! These peoples go peaceably to the ballot-box together to decide upon the destiny of government! These peoples melt into an harmonious citizenry! These peoples have and exercise mutual confidence, esteem and appreciation of their common rights! These peoples *dissolve into one people!* The bare statement of the case condemns it as impracticable, illusory, in the extreme. And, yet, these two peoples, so different in character, in education and material condition, were turned loose to enjoy the same benefits in common—to be one! And the *wise men* of the nation—as, Tourgee's *Fool* ironically names them— thought they were legislating for the best; thought they were doing their duty. And, so, having made the people free, and equal before the law, and given them the ballot with which to settle their disputes, the *"wise men"* left the people to live in peace if they could, and to cut each other's throats if they could not. That they should have proceeded to cut each other's throats was as natural as it is for day to follow night.

I do not desire to be understood as inveighing against the manumission of the slave or the enfranchisement of the new-made free man. To do so, would be most paradoxical on my part, who was born a slave and spent the first nine years of my life in that most unnatural condition. What I do inveigh against, is the unequal manner in which the colored people were pitted against the white people; the placing of these helpless people absolutely in the power of this hereditary foeman—more absolutely in their power, at their mercy, than under the merciless system of slavery, when sordid interest dictated a modicum of humanity and care in treatment. And I arraign the "Reconstruction policy" as one of the hollowest pieces of perfidy ever perpetrated upon an innocent, helpless people; and in the treatment of the issues growing out of that policy, I arraign the dominant party of the time for base ingratitude, subterfuge and hypocrisy to its black partisan allies.

With the whole power of the government at its back, and with a Constitution so amended as to extend the amplest protection to the new-made citizen, it left him to the inhuman mercy of men whose uncurbed passions, whose deeds of lawlessness and defiance, pale into virtues the ferocity of Cossack warfare. And, for this treachery, for leaving this people alone and single-handed, to fight an enemy born in the lap of self-confidence, and rocked in the cradle of arrogance and cruelty, the "party of great moral ideas" must go down to history amid the hisses and the execrations of honest men in spite of its good deeds. These is not one extenuating circumstance to temper the indignation of him who believes in justice and humanity.

As I stand before the thirteen bulky volumes, comprising the "Ku Klux Conspiracy," being the report of the "Joint Select Committee, to inquire into the condition of affairs in the late Insurrectionary States," on the part of the Senate and House of Representatives of the United States, reported February 19, 1872, my blood runs cold at the merciless chronicle of murder and outrage, of defiance, inhumanity and barbarity on the one hand, and usurpation and tyranny on the other.

If the shot upon Fort Sumter was treason, what shall we call the bloody conflict which the white men of the South have waged against the Constitutional amendments from 1866 to the murder of innocent citizens at Danville, Virginia, in 1883—even unto the present time? If the shot upon Fort Sumter drew down upon the South the indignation and the vengeance of the Federal government, putting father against son, and brother against brother, what shall we say the Federal Government should have done to put a period to the usurpation and the murders of these leagues of horror?

The entire adult male population of the South, though no longer in armed "Rebellion," appeared to be in league against the government of the United States. The arm of State authority was paralyzed, the operation of courts of justice was suspended, lawlessness and individual license walked abroad, and anarchy, pure and simple, prevailed. Under the name of the "Ku Klux Klan," the South was bound by the following oath, ironclad, paradoxical and enigmatical as it is:

I, [name] before the great immaculate Judge of heaven and earth, and upon the Holy Evangelists of Almighty God, do, of my own free will and accord, subscribe to the following sacred, binding obligation:

I. I am on the side of justice and humanity and constitutional liberty, as bequeathed to us by our forefathers in its original purity.

II. I reject and oppose the principles of the radical party.

III. I pledge aid to a brother of the Ku-Klux Klan in sickness, distress, or pecuniary embarrassments. Females, friends, widows, and their households shall be the special object of my care and protection.

IV. Should I ever divulge, or cause to be divulged, any of the secrets of this order, or any of the foregoing obligations, I must meet with the fearful punishment of death and traitor's doom, which is death, death, death, at the hands of the brethren.

Murderers, incendiaries, midnight raiders on the "side of justice, humanity and Constitutional liberty"! Let us see what kind of "justice, humanity and Constitutional liberty" is meant. In Volume I, page 21, I find the following:

Taking these statements from official sources, showing the prevalence of this organization in every one of the late insurrectionary States and in Kentucky, it is difficult now, with the light that has recently been thrown upon its history, to realize that even its existence has been for so long a mooted question in the public mind. Especially is this remarkable in view of the effects that are disclosed by some of this documentary evidence to have been produced by it. That it was used as a means of intimidating and murdering negro voters during the presidential election of 1868, the testimony in the Louisiana and other contested-election cases already referred to clearly establishes.

Taking the results in Louisiana alone as an instance, the purpose of the organization at that time, whatever it may have been at its origin, could hardly be doubted.

A member of the committee which took that testimony thus sums it up:

The testimony shows that over 2,000 persons were killed, wounded, and otherwise injured in that State within a few weeks prior to the presidential election; that half the State was overrun by violence; midnight raids, secret murders, and open riot kept the people in constant terror until the Republicans surrendered all claims, and then the election was carried by the Democracy. The parish of Orleans contained 29,910 voters, 15,020 black. In the spring of 1868 that parish gave 13,973 republican votes. In the fall of 1868 it gave Grant 1,178, a falling off of 12,795 votes. Riots prevailed for weeks, sweeping the city of New Orleans, and filling it with scenes of blood, and Ku-Klux notices were scattered through the city warning the colored men not to vote. In Caddo there were 2,987 Republicans. In the spring of 1868 they carried the parish. In the fall they gave Grant one vote. Here also there were bloody riots.

But the most remarkable case is that of St. Landry, a planting parish on the River Teche. Here the Republicans had a registered majority of 1,071 votes. In the spring of 1868 they carried the parish by 678. In the fall they gave Grant no vote, not one; while the democrats cast 4,787, the full vote of the parish, for Seymour and Blair.

Here occurred one of the bloodiest riots on record, in which the Ku-Klux killed and wounded over two hundred Republicans, hunting and chasing them for two days and nights through fields and swamps. Thirteen captives were taken from the jail and shot. A pile of twenty-five dead bodies was found half buried in the woods. Having conquered the Republicans, killed and driven off the white leaders, the Ku-Klux captured the masses, marked them with badges of red flannel, enrolled them in clubs, led them to the polls, made them vote the Democratic ticket, and then gave them certificates of the fact.

It is not my purpose to weary the reader with tedious citations from the cumbersome reports of the "Ku Klux conspiracy." Those reports are accessible to the reading public. They tell the bloody story of the terrible miscarriage of the "Reconstruction policy;" they show how cruel men can be under conditions favorable to unbridled license, undeterred by the strong arm of constituted authority; they show how helpless the freed people were; how ignorant, how easily led by unscrupulous adventurers *pretending to be friends* and how easily murdered and overawed by veterans inured to the dangers and the toils of war; and, lastly, they show how powerless was the national government to protect its citizens' rights, specifically defined by the Federal constitution. *Was*, do I say? It is as powerless to day!

In this brief review, then, of the history and present political condition of the American Negro I cannot omit, though I shall not detail, the horrors of the Ku Klux period. They are a link in the chain: and though today's links are different in form and guise, *the chain is the same.* Let the reader, then, be a little patient at being reminded of things which he has perhaps forgotten.

CHAPTER VIII

The Nation Surrenders

━━━◄❦►━━━

The mind sickens in contemplating the mistakes of the "Reconstruction policy;" and the revolting peculation and crime—which went hand in hand from 1867-8 to 1876, bankrupting and terrorizing those unfortunate States—plunging them into all but anarchy, pure and simple.

A parallel to the terror which walked abroad in the South from 1866, down to 1876, and which is largely dominant in that section even unto the present hour, must be sought for in other lands than our own, where the iron hand of the tyrant, seated upon a throne, cemented with a thousand years of usurpation and the blood of millions of innocent victims, presses hard upon the necks of the high and the backs of the low; we must turn to the dynastic villanies of the house of Orleans or of Stuart, or that prototype of all that is tyrannical, sordid and inhuman, the Czar of all the Russias. The "Invisible Empire," with its "Knights of the White Camelia," was as terrible as the "Empire" which Marat, Danton and Robespierre made for themselves, with this difference: the "Knights of the White Camelia" were assassins and marauders who murdered and terrorized in defiance of all laws, human or divine, though claiming allegiance to both; while the Frenchmen regarded themselves as the lawful authority of the land and rejected utterly the Divine or "higher law." The one murdered men as highwaymen do, while the other murdered them under the cover of law and in the name of *Liberty*, in whose name, as

Madame Roland exclaimed on the scaffold of revolutionary vengeance, so many crimes are perpetrated! The one murdered kings and aristocrats to unshackle the limbs of the proletariat of France; the other murdered the proletariat of the South to rerivet their chains upon the wretched survivors. And each class of murders proclaimed that it was actuated by the motive of *justice and humanity*. Liberty was the grand inspiration that steeled the arm and hardened the heart of each of the avengers!

And thus it has been in all the history of murder and plunder. Liberty! the People! these are the sacred objects with which tyrants cloak their usurpations, and which assassins plead in extenuation of their brazen disregard of life, of virtue, of all that is dear and sacred to the race. The dagger of Brutus and the sword of Cromwell, were they not drawn in the name of Liberty—the People? The guillotine of the French Commune and the derringer of J. Wilkes Booth, were they not inspired by Liberty—the People?

The innocent blood which has been spilt in the name of liberty and the people, which has served the purposes of tyranny and riveted upon the people most galling chains, "would float a navy."

By the side of the robbery, the embezzlement, the depletion of the treasury of South Carolina, and the imposition of ruinous and unnecessary taxation upon the people of that state by the Carpet-Bag harpies, aided and abetted by the ignorant negroes whom our government had not given time to shake the dust of the cornfield from their feet before it invited them to seats in the chambers of legislature, we must place the heartless butcheries of Hamburgh and Ellenton.

By the side of the misgovernment, the honeycomb of corruption in which the Carpet-Bag government of Louisiana reveled, we must place the universal lawlessness which that state witnessed from 1867 to 1876.

The whole gamut of states could be run with the same deplorable, the same sickening conclusion.

The Federal authority had created the wildest confusion and retired to watch the fire-brand. The "wise men" of the nation had made possible a system of government in which robbery and murder were to contend for the mastery, in which organized ig-norance and organized brigandage were to contend for the right to rule *and* to ruin.

It is not complimentary to the white men of the South that their organized brigandage proved to be more stubborn, more far-sighted than was unorganized ignorance. In a warfare of this disreputable nature very little honor can be accorded to the vic-torious party, be he brigand or ignoramus. The warfare is abso-lutely devoid of principle, and, therefore, victory, any way it is twisted, is supremely dishonorable.

The South, therefore, although she rooted out the incubus of *carpet-baggism* (one of the most noxious plants that ever blos-somed in the garden of any nascent society), and stifled the liberties and immunities of a whole people, turning their new-found joy into sadness and mourning—although the South suc-ceeded in accomplishing these results, she lies prostrate to-day, feared by her fellow-citizens, who will not trust her with power, and shunned by the industrious aliens who seek our shores, be-cause they will not become members of a society in which individ-ualism and absolutism are the supreme law—for was it not to escape these parasites that they expatriated themselves from the shores of the Volga, the Danube and the Rhine? Men will not make their homes among people who, spurning the accepted canons of justice and the courts of law, make themselves a com-munity of *banditti*. Thus, the South lies prostrate, staggering be-neath a load of illiteracy sufficient to paralyze the energies of any people; dwelling in the midst of usurpation, where law is suspended and individual license is the standard authority; where criminals and suspected criminals are turned over to the rude mercy of mobs, masked and irresponsible; where caste corrupts every rivulet that issues from the fountain of aspiration or of chastity;* where no man is allowed to think or act for himself who does not conform his thoughts and shape his actions to suit the censorious and haughty *dictum* of the dominant class. "You must think as we think and act as we act, or you must go!" This is the law of the South.

In each of the late rebellious states the ballotbox has been closed against the black man. To reach it he is compelled to brave the muzzles of a thousand rifles in the hands of silent sentinels who esteem a human life as no more sacred than the serpent that drags his tortuous length among the grasses of the field, and whose head mankind is enjoined to crush.

The thirteenth, fourteenth and fifteenth amendments to the Federal constitution which grew out of the public sentiment created by thirty long years of agitation of the abolitionists and of the "emancipation proclamation"—issued as a war measure by President Lincoln—are no longer regarded as fundamental by the South. The beneficiaries of those amendments have failed in every instance to enjoy the benefits that were, presumably, intended to be conferred.

---

* "Southerners fire up terribly, as has been noted in these columns again and again, when the subject of intermarriage between whites and negroes is discussed. But the terrible state of immorality which exists there, involving white men and colored women, is something upon which the papers of that region are silent as a rule. Not so the grand jury that met recently at Madison, Ga., which thus spoke out in its presentment with all plainness of the Old Testament:

"After several days of laborious investigation we have found the moral state of our country in a fair condition, and the freedom of our community from any great criminal offenses is a subject for congratulation to our people. But the open and shameless cohabitation of white men with negro women in our community cries to heaven for abatement. This crime in its nature has been such as to elude our grasp owing to the limited time of our session. It is poisoning the fountains of our social life; it is ruining and degrading our young men, men who would scorn to have imputation put on them of equalization with negroes, but who have, nevertheless, found the lowest depths of moral depravity in this unnatural shame of their lives."

"The despatch chronicling the presentment adds: 'The reading of this presentment in court aroused a great feeling of indignation among men who declare that the private affairs of the people should not be intruded upon.' It strikes the Northern mind that until these 'private affairs' do not need to be 'intruded upon,' Southern newspapers and Southern clergymen would with better grace bottle up their indignation upon the terrible evils likely to result from the legitimate intermarriage of the two races."—*Newspaper waif.*

These laws—having passed both branches of the Federal legislature, having received the approval and signature of the Chief Executive of the nation, and having been ratified by a majority of the states composing the sisterhood of states—these laws are no longer binding upon the people of the South, who fought long and desperately to prevent the possibility of their enactment; and they no longer benefit, if they ever did, the people in whose interest they were incorporated in the *Magna Charta* of American liberty; *while the Central authority which originated them, has, through the Supreme Court, declared nugatory, null and void all supplementary legislation based upon those laws, as far as the government of the United States is concerned!* The whole question has been remanded to the legislatures of the several states! The Federal Union has left to the usurped governments of the South the adjudication of rights which the South fought four years in honorable warfare to make impossible, and which it has since the war exhausted the catalogue of infamy and lawlessness to make of no force or effect. The fate of the lamb has been left to the mercy of the lion and the tiger.

The "party of great moral ideas," having emancipated the slave, and enfranchised disorganized ignorance and poverty, finally finished its mission, relinquished its right to the respect and confidence of mankind when, in 1876, it abandoned all effort to enforce the provisions of the war amendments. That party stands today for organized corruption, while its opponent stands for organized brigandage. The black man, who was betrayed by his party and murdered by the opponents of his party, is absolved from all allegiance which *gratitude* may have dictated, and is to-day free to make conditions the best possible with any faction which will insure him in his right to "life, liberty and the pursuit of happiness."

The black men of the United States are, today, free to form whatever alliances wisdom dictates, to make sure their position in the social and civil system of which, in the wise providence of a just God, they are a factor, for better or for worse.

CHAPTER IX

Political Independence of the Negro

❖————◄◖◅◌☺◌◄◖————❖

The following chapter is, in the main, a reproduction of an address delivered by me before the Colored Press Association, in the city of Washington, June 27, 1882:—

In addressing myself to a consideration of the subject: "The colored man as an Independent Force in our Politics," I come at once to one of the vital principles underlying American citizenship of the colored man in a peculiar manner. Upon this question hang all the conditions of man as a free moral agent, as an intelligent reasoning being; as a man thoughtful for the best interests of his country, of his individual interests, and of the interests of those who must take up the work of republican government when the present generation has passed away. When I say that this question is of a most complex and perplexing nature, I only assert what is known of all men.

I would not forget that the arguments for and against independent action on our part are based upon two parties or sets of principles. Principles are inherent in government by the people, and parties are engines created by the people through which to voice the principles they espouse. Parties have divided on one line in this country from the beginning of our national existence to the present time. All other issues merge into two distinct ones— the question of a strong Federal Government, as enunciated by Alexander Hamilton, and maintained by the present Republican party, and the question of the rights and powers of the States, as enunciated by Thomas Jefferson, and as maintained by the present Democratic party,—called the "party of the people," but in fact the party of oligarchy, bloodshed, violence and oppression. The Republican party won its first great victory on the inherent weakness of the Democratic party on the question of Human Rights and the right of the Federal Government to protect itself from the assumption, the aggression, the attempted usurpation, of the States, and it has maintained its supremacy for so long a time as to lead to the supposition that it will rule until such time as it shall fall to pieces of itself because of internal decay and exterior cancers. There does not appear to exist sufficient vitality outside of the Republican party to keep its members loyal to the people or honest to the government. The loyal legislation which would be occasioned by dread of loss of power, and the administration of the government in the most economical form, are wanting, because of the absence of an honest, healthy opposing party.

But it is not my purpose to dwell upon the mechanism of parties, but rather to show why colored Americans should be independent voters, independent citizens, independent men. To this end I am led to lay it down: (1.) That an independent voter must be intelligent, must comprehend the science of government, and be versed in the history of governments and of men; (2.) That an independent voter must be not only a citizen versed in government, but one loyal to his country, and generous and forbearing with his fellow-citizens, not looking always to the word and the act, but looking sometimes to the undercurrent which actuates these—to the presence of immediate interest, which is always strong in human nature, to the love of race, and to the love of section, which comes next to the love of country.

Our country is great not only in mineral and cereal resources, in numbers, and in accumulated wealth, but great in extent of territory, and in multiplicity of interests, out-growing from peculiarities of locality, race, and the education of the people. Thus the people of the North and East and West are given to farming, manufacturing, and speculation, making politics a subordinate, not a leading interest; they are consequently wealthy, thrifty and contented: while the people of the South, still in the shadow of defeat in the bloodiest and most tremendous conflict since the Napoleonic wars, are divided sharply into two classes, and given almost exclusively to the pursuits of agriculture and hatred of one another. The existence of this state of things is most disastrous in its nature, and deplorable in its results. It is a barrier against the progress of that section and alien to the spirit and subversive of the principles of our free institutions.

It is in the South that the largest number of our people live; it is there that they encounter the greatest hardships; it is there the problem of their future usefulness as American citizens must have full and satisfactory, or disastrous and disheartening demonstration. Consequently, the colored statesman and the colored editor must turn their attention to the South and make that field the center of speculation, deduction and practical application. We all understand the conditions of society in that section and the causes which have produced them, and, while not forgetting the causes, it is a common purpose to alter the existing conditions, so that they may conform to the logic of the great Rebellion and the spirit and letter of the Federal Constitution. It is not surprising, therefore, that, as an humble worker in the interest of my race and the common good, I have decided views as to the course best to be pursued by our people in that section, and the fruits likely to spring from a consistent advocacy of such views.

I may stand alone in the opinion that the best interests of the race and the best interests of the country will be conserved by building up a bond of union between the white people and the negroes of the South—advocating the doctrine that the interests of the white and the interests of the colored people are one and the same; that the legislation which affects the one will affect the other; that the good which comes to the one should come to the other, and that, as one people, the evils which blight the hopes of the one blight the hopes of the other; I say, I may stand alone among colored men in the belief that harmony of sentiment between the blacks and whites of the country, in so far forth as it tends to honest division and healthy opposition, is natural and necessary, but I speak that which is a conviction as strong as the Stalwart idea of diversity between Black and White, which has so crystallized the opinion of the race.

It is not safe in a republican form of government that clannishness should exist, either by compulsory or voluntary reason; it is not good for the government, it is not good for the individual. A government like ours is like unto a household. Difference of opinion on non-essentials is wholesome and natural, but upon the fundamental idea incorporated in the Declaration of Independence and re-affirmed in the Federal Constitution the utmost unanimity should prevail. That all men are born equal, so far as the benefits of government extend; that each and every man is justly entitled to the enjoyment of life, liberty and the pursuit of happiness, so long as these benign benefits be not forfeited by infraction upon the rights of others; that freedom of thought and unmolested expression of honest conviction and the right to make these effective through the sacred medium of a fair vote and an honest count, are God-given and not to be curtailed—these are the foundations of republican government; these are the foundations of our institutions; these are the birthright of every American citizen; these are the guarantees which make men free and independent and great.

The colored man must rise to a full conception of his citizenship before he can make his citizenship effective. It is a fatality to create or foster clannishness in a government like ours. Assimilation of sentiment must be the property of the German, the Irish, the English, the Anglo-African, and all other racial elements that contribute to the formation of the American type of citizen. The moment you create a caste standard, the moment you recognize the existence of such, that moment republican government stands beneath the sword of Damocles, the vitality of its being becomes vitiated and endangered. If this be true, the American people have grave cause for apprehension. The Anglo-African element of our population is classed off by popular sentiment, and kept so. It is for the thoughtful, the honest, the calm but resolute men of the race to mould the sentiment of the masses, lift them up into the broad sunlight of freedom. Ignorance, superstition, prejudice, and intolerance are elements in our nature born of the malign institution of servitude. No fiat of government can eradicate these. As they were the slow growth, the gradual development of long years of inhuman conditions, so they must be eliminated by the slow growth of years of favorable conditions. Let us recognize these facts as facts, and labor honestly to supplant them with more wholesome, more cheering realities. The Independent colored man, like the Independent white man, is an American citizen who does his own thinking. When some one else thinks for him he ceases to be an intelligent citizen and becomes a dangerous dupe —dangerous to himself, dangerous to the State.

It is not to be expected now that the colored voters will continue to maintain that unanimity of idea and action characteristic of them when the legislative halls of States resounded with the clamor of law-makers of their creation, and when their breath flooded or depleted State treasuries. The conditions are different now. They find themselves citizens without a voice in the shapement of legislation; tax-payers without representation; men without leadership masterful enough to force respect from inferior numbers in some States, or to hold the balance of power in others. They find themselves at the mercy of a relentless public opinion which tolerates but does not respect their existence as a voting force; but which, on the contrary, while recognizing their right to the free exercise of the suffrage, forbids such exercise at the point of the shotgun of the assassin, whom it not only nerves but shields in the perpetration of his lawless and infamous crimes. And why is this? Why is it that the one hundred and twenty thousand black voters of South Carolina allow the eighty thousand white voters of that State to grind the life out of them by laws more odious, more infamous, more tyrannical and subversive of manhood than any which depopulate the governments of the old world? Is it because the white man is the created viceregent of government? The Scriptures affirm that all are sprung from one parental stem. Is it because he is the constitutionally invested oligarch of government? The magna charta of our liberties affirms that "all men are created equal." Is it because the law of the land reserves unto him the dominance of power? The preamble of the Federal Constitution declares that "We" and not "I," constitute "the people of the United States." If the law of God and the law of man agree in the equality of right of man, explain to me the cause which keeps a superior force in subjection to a minority. Look to the misgovernment of the Reconstruction period for the answer—misgovernment by white men and black men who were lifted into a "little brief authority" by a mighty but unwieldy voting force. That black man who connived at and shared in the corruption in the South which resulted in the subversion of the majority rule, is a traitor to his race and his country, wherever he may now be eking out a precarious and inglorious existence, and I have nothing to heap upon his head but the curses, the execrations of an injured people. Like Benedict Arnold he should seek a garret in the desert of population, living unnoticed and without respect, where he might die without arousing the contempt of his people.

The love of Liberty carries with it the courage to preserve it from encroachments from without and from contempt from within. A people in whom the love of liberty is in-born cannot be enslaved, though they may be exterminated by superior force and intelligence, as in the case of the poor Indian of our own land —a people who, two hundred years ago, spread their untamed hordes from the icebergs of Maine to the balmy sunland of Florida. But to-day where are they? Their love of freedom and valorous defense of priority of ownership of our domain have caused them to be swept from the face of the earth. Had they possessed intelligence with their more than Spartan courage, the wave of extermination could never have rolled over them forever. As a man I admire the unconquerable heroism and fortitude of the Indian. So brave a race of people were worthy a nobler and a happier destiny. As an American citizen, I feel it born in my nature to share in fullest measure all that is American. I sympathize in all the hopes, aspirations and fruitions of my country. There is no pulsation in the animated frame of my native land which does not thrill my nature. There is no height of glory we may reach as a government in which I should not feel myself individually lifted; and there is no depth of degradation to which we may fall to which I should not feel myself individually dragged. In a word, I am an American citizen. I have a heritage in each and every provision incorporated in the Constitution of my country, and should this heritage be attempted to be filched from me by any man or body of men, I should deem the provocation sufficiently grievous to stake even life in defense of it. I would plant every colored man in this country on a platform of this nature—to think for himself, to speak for himself, to act for himself. This is the ideal citizen of an ideal government such as ours is modelled to become. This is my conception of the colored man as an independent force in our politics. To aid in lifting our people to this standard, is one of the missions which I have mapped out for my life-work. I may be sowing the seed that will ripen into disastrous results, but I don't think so. My conception of republican government does not lead me to a conclusion so inconsistent with my hopes, my love of my country and of my race.

I look upon my race in the South and I see that they are helplessly at the mercy of a popular prejudice outgrowing from a previous condition of servitude; I find them clothed in the garments of citizenship by the Federal Government and opposed in the enjoyment of it by their equals, not their superiors, in the benefits of government; I find that the government which conferred the right of citizenship is powerless, or indisposed, to force respect for its own enactments; I find that these people, left to the mercy of their enemies, alone and defenseless, and without judicious leadership, are urged to preserve themselves loyal to the men and to the party which have shown themselves unable to extend to them substantial protection; I find that these people, alone in their struggles of doubt and of prejudice, are surrounded by a public opinion powerful to create and powerful to destroy; I find them poor in culture and poor in worldly substance, and dependent for the bread they eat upon those they antagonize politically. As a consequence, though having magnificent majorities, they have no voice in shaping the legislation which is too often made an engine to oppress them; though performing the greatest amount of labor, they suffer from overwork and insufficient remuneration; though having the greater number of children, the facilities of education are not as ample or as good as those provided for the whites out of the common fund, nor have they means to supply from private avenues the benefits of education denied them by the State. Now, what is the solution of this manifold and grievous state of things? Will it come by standing solidly opposed to the sentiment, the culture, the statesmanship, and the possession of the soil and wealth of the South? Let the history of the past be spread before the eyes of a candid and thoughtful people; let the bulky roll of misgovernment, incompetence, and blind folly be enrolled on the one hand, and then turn to the terrors of the midnight assassin and the lawless deeds which desecrate the sunlight of noontide, walking abroad as a phantom armed with the desperation of the damned!

I maintain the idea that the preservation of our liberties, the consummation of our citizenship, must be conserved and matured, not by standing alone and apart, sullen as the melancholy Dane, but by imbibing all that is American, entering into the life and spirit of our institutions, spreading abroad in sentiment, feeling the full force of the fact that while we are classed as Africans, just as the Germans are classed as Germans we are in all things American citizens, American freemen. Since we have tried the idea of political unanimity let us now try other ideas, ideas more in consonance with the spirit of our institution. There is no strength in a union that enfeebles. Assimilation, a melting into the corporate body, having no distinction from others, equally the recipients of government—this is to be the independent man, be his skin tanned by the torrid heat of Africa, or bleached by the eternal snows of the Caucasus. To preach the independence of the colored man is to preach his Americanization. The shackles of slavery have been torn from his limbs by the stern arbitrament of arms; the shackles of political enslavement, of ignorance, and of popular prejudice must be broken on the wheels of ceaseless study and the facility with which he becomes absorbed into the body of the people. To aid himself is his first duty if he believes that he is here to stay, and not a probationer for the land of his forefathers—a land upon which he has no other claim than one of sentiment.

What vital principle affecting our citizenship is championed by the National Republican party of to-day? Is it a fair vote and an honest count? Measure our strength in the South and gaze upon the solitary expression of our citizenship in the halls of the National Legislature. The fair vote which we cast for Rutherford B. Hayes seemed to have incurred the enmity of that chief Executive, and he and his advisers turned the colored voters of the South over to the bloodthirsty minority of that section.

The Republican party has degenerated into an ignoble scramble for place and power. It has forgotten the prinicples for which Sumner contended, and for which Lincoln died. It betrayed the cause for which Douglass, Garrison and others labored, in the blind policy it pursued in reconstructing the rebellious States. It made slaves freemen and freemen slaves in the same breath by conferring the franchise and withholding the guarantees to insure its exercise; it betrayed its trust in permitting thousands of innocent men to be slaughtered without declaring the South in rebellion, and in pardoning murders, whom tardy justice had consigned to a felon's dungeon. It is even now powerless to insure an honest expression of the vote of the colored citizen. For these things, I do not deem it binding upon colored men further to support the Republican party when other more advantageous affiliations can be formed. And what of the Bourbon Democratic party? There has not been, there is not now, nor will there ever be, any good thing in it for the colored man. Bourbon Democracy is a curse to our land. Any party is a curse which arrays itself in opposition to human freedom, to the universal brotherhood of man. No colored man can ever claim truthfully to be a Bourbon Democrat. It is a fundamental impossibility. But he can be an independent, a progressive Democrat.

The hour has arrived when thoughtful colored men should cease to put their faith upon broken straws; when they should cease to be the willing tools of a treacherous and corrupt party; when they should cease to support men and measures which do not benefit them or the race; when they should cease to be duped by one faction and shot by the other. The time has fully arrived when they should have their position in parties more fully defined, and when, by the ballot which they hold, they should force more respect for the rights of life and property.

To do this, they must adjust themselves to the altered condition which surrounds them. They must make for themselves a place to stand. In the politics of the country the colored vote must be made as uncertain a quantity as the German and Irish vote. The color of their skin must cease to be an index to their political creed. They must think less of "the party" and more of themselves; give less heed to a name and more heed to principles.

The black men and white men of the South have a common destiny. Circumstances have brought them together and so interwoven their interests that nothing but a miracle can dissolve the link that binds them. It is, therefore, to their mutual disadvantage that anything but sympathy and good will should prevail. A reign of terror means a stagnation of all the energies of the people and a corruption of the fountains of law and justice.

The colored men of the South must cultivate more cordial relations with the white men of the South. They must, by a wise policy, hasten the day when politics shall cease to be the shibboleth that creates perpetual warfare. The citizen of a State is far more sovereign than the citizen of the United States. The State is a real, tangible reality; a thing of life and power; while the United States is, purely, an abstraction—a thing that no man has successfully defined, although many, wise in their way and in their own conceit, have philosophized upon it to their own satisfaction. The metaphysical polemics of men learned in the science of republican government, covering volume upon volume of "debates," the legislation of ignoramuses, styled statesmen, and the "strict" and "liberal" construction placed upon their work by the judicial *magi*, together with a long and disastrous rebellion, to the cruel arbitrament of which the question had been, as was finally hoped, in the last resort, submitted, have failed, all and each, to define that visionary thing the so-called Federal government, and its just rights and powers. As Alexander Hamilton and Thomas Jefferson left it, so it is to-day, a bone of contention, a red flag in the hands of the political matadors of one party to infuriate those of the other parties.

No: it is time that the colored voter learned to leave his powerless "protectors" and take care of himself. Let every one read, listen, think, reform his own ideas of affairs in his own locality; let him be less interested in the continual wars of national politics than in the interests of his own town and county and state; let him make friends of the mammon of unrighteousness of his own neighborhood, so far as to take an intelligent part among his neighbors, white and black, and vote for the men and for the party that will do the best for him and his race, and best conserve the interest of his vicinity. Let there be no aim of *solidifying* the colored vote; the massing of black means the massing of white by contrast. Individual colored men—and many of them—have done wonders in self-elevation; but there can be no general elevation of the colored men of the South until they use their voting power in independent local affairs with some discrimination more reasonable than an obstinate clinging to a party name. When the colored voters differ among themselves and are to be found on *both sides* of local political contests, they will begin to find themselves of some political importance; their votes will be sought, cast, *and counted.*

And this is the key to the whole situation; let them make themselves a part of the people. It will take time, patience, intelligence, courage; but it can be done: and until it is done their path will lie in darkness and perhaps in blood.

CHAPTER X

Solution of the Political Problem

I have no faith in parties. In monarchical and imperial governments they are always manipulated by royal boobies, who are in
turn manipulated by their empty-pated favorites and their women
of soporific virtue; while in republics they are always manipulated by demagogues, tricksters, and corruptionists, who figure in
the newspapers as "bosses," "heelers" and "sluggers," and in
history as statesmen, senators and representatives. These gentlemen, who *rule* our government and *ruin* our people, comprise what
Mr. Matthew Arnold recently termed the "remnant" which should
be permitted to run things to suit themselves, the people, the great
mass, being incapable of taking care of themselves and the complex machinery of government. Of course, Mr. Arnold, who is
necessarily very British in his ideas of government, intended that
the "remnant" he had in his "mind's eye," should comprise men
of the most exalted character and intelligence, the very things
which keep them out of the gutters of politics. Men of exalted
character are expected in our country to attend to their own concerns, not the concerns of the people, and to give the "boys" a
chance; while the men of exalted intelligence are, by reason of
the great industry and seclusiveness necessary to their work, too
much wedded to their books and their quiet modes of life to rush
into ward meetings and contend for political preferment with the
"Mikes" and "Jakes" who make their bread and butter out of
the spoils and peculations of office. A Clay or Webster, a Seward

or Sumner, sometimes gets into politics, but it is by accident. There is not enough money in our politics to cause honest men to make it an object, while the corruption frequently necessary to maintain a political position, is so disgusting as to deter honest men from making it a business.

A love of power easily degenerates from patriotism into treason or tyranny, or both. As it is easier to fall from virtue to vice than it is to rise from vice to virtue, so it is easier to fall from patriotism than to rise to it.

Before the war the men of the South engaged, at first, in politics as an elegant pastime. They had plenty of leisure and plenty of money. They did not take to literature and science, because these pursuits require severe work and more or less of a strong bias, for a thorough exposition of their profound penetralia. It may be, too, that their assumed patrician sensitiveness shrank from entering into competition with the plebeian fellows who had to study hard and write voluminously for a few pennies to keep soul and body together. And your Southern grandees, before the war, were not compelled to drudge for a subsistence; they had to take little thought for the morrow. Their vast landed estates and black slaves were things that did not fluctuate; under the effective supervision of the viperous slave-driver the black Samson rose before the coming of the sun, and the land, nature's own flower garden and man's inalienable heritage, brought forth golden corn and snowy cotton in their season. Southern intelligence expended its odors in the avenues where brilliance, not profundity, was the passport to popularity. Hence, Southern hospitality (giving to others that which had been deliberately stolen) became almost as proverbial in the *polite* circles of America and Europe as the long established suavity and condescension of the French. And even unto the present time the hospitality of the South, shorn of its profuseness and grandiloquence, is frequently the theme of newspaper hacks and magazine penny-a-liners. But the shadow alone remains; the substance has departed—"There are no birds in last year's nest."

If the literary reputation of the United States had been rated, up to the close of the Rebellion, on the contributions of Southern men—fiction, prose and poetry, science, art, and invention—the polite nations of the world would have regarded us as a nation of semi-barbarians. But, happily, the rugged genius of New England made up then and makes up now for the poverty of literary effort on the part of the South. True, a few men since the war have placed the South in a better light; but even their work, as an index of Southern genius, is regarded as highly precocious and tentative.

The South has yet to demonstrate that she has capacity for high literary effort. In the process of that demonstration, I am fully persuaded that the Anglo-African—with his brilliant wit and humor, his highly imaginative disposition and his innate fondness for literary pursuits—will contribute largely to give the South an enviable and honorable position.

What the South lacked in literary effort before the war she made up in a magnificent galaxy of meteoric statesmen, who rushed into politics with the instinct of ducks taking to water, and who were forgotten, in the majority of cases, before they had run out their ephemeral career. A few names have survived the earthquake, and are remembered for their cleverness rather than their depth. A few more decades, and they will be remembered only by the curious student who plods his weary way through the labyrinth of Congressional records and the musty archives of States, seeking for data of times which long ago passed into the hazy vista of history and romance. Before the war the Southern man of leisure took to politics more as a pastime than as a serious business. But as the pastime was agreeable, and as it gave additional weight and distinction, all those who could, strived to make it appear that they were men of importance in the Nation. They were

largely a nation of politicians, always brilliant, shallow, belli-
cose and dogmatic, as ready to decide an argument with the shotgun or saber as with reason and logic.

This was the temper of the people who rushed into the war with
the confidence of a schoolboy and who limped out like a man
overtaken in his gymnastic exercise by a paralytic stroke. The war
taught the South a very useful lesson, but did not sufficiently convince it that it was preëminently a supercilious, arrogant people,
who did not and do not possess all the virtue, intelligence, and
courage of the country; that its stock of these prime elements is
woefully small considering the long years it had posed as America's own patrician class.

But when the war was over, and the Southern nobility turned
its thoughts once more to social arrogance and political dominion,
it found that Othello's occupation was entirely gone. A revolution had swept over the country more iconoclastic and merciless
than that which followed in the wake of the French revolution
nearly a hundred years before. The bottom rail had been vio-
lently placed upon the top; industrial adjustments had been so
completely metamorphosed as to defy detection; while the basis
and the method of political representation and administration
had been so altered as to confound both the old and the new
forces.

Aside from the ignorance of the black citizens and the insatiate
greed and unscrupulousness of their carpet-bag leaders—a band
of vultures more voracious and depraved than any which ever before imposed upon and abused the confidence of a credulous
people—the white men of the South had been educated to regard
themselves as, naturally, the factors of power and the colored
people as, naturally, the subject class, no factor at all. It was these
two things which produced that exhibition of barbarity on the
part of the South and impotence on the part of the government
which make us go to Roumania and the Byzantine court for fit
parallel.

But, as I have said, a love of power easily degenerates into treason. If we may not call the violence, the assassinations, which have disgraced the South, *treason* by what fitter name, pray, shall we call it? If the nullification of the letter and spirit of the amendments of the Federal Constitution by the conquered South was not renewed *treason*, what was it? What is it?

The white men of the South, to the "manor born," having shown their superiority in the superlative excellencies of murder, usurpation and robbery (and I maintain they have gone further in the execution of these infamies than was true of the Negro-Carpet-bag *bacchanalia*); having made majorities dwindle into iotas and vaulted themselves into power at the point of the shot gun and dagger (regular bandit style); having made laws which discriminate odiously against one class while giving the utmost immunity to the other; having, after doing these things, modeled the government they rule upon the pro-slavery doctrine that it is a "white man's government"—having had time to become sobered, the white men of the South should be open to reason, if not to conviction.

The black men of the South know full well that they were disfranchised by illegal and violent methods; they know that laws are purposely framed to defraud and to oppress them. This is dangerous knowledge, dangerous to the black and the white man. It will be decided by one of two courses—wise and judicious statesmanship or bloody and disastrous insurrection. When men are wronged they appeal either to the arbitrament of reason or of violence. No man who loves his country would sanction violence in the adjudication of rights save as a last resort. Reason is the safest tribunal before which to arraign injustice and wrong; but it is not always possible to reach this tribunal.

The black and white citizens of the South must alter the lines which have divided them since the close of the war. They are, essentially, one people, and should be mutual aids instead of mutual hindrances to each other. By "one people" I don't wish to be understood as implying that the white and black man are one in an ethnological, but a generic sense, having a common origin. Living in the same communities, pursuing identical avocations, and subject to the same fundamental laws, however these may differ in construction and application in the several States, it is as much, if not even more, the interest of the white man that the black should be given every possible opportunity to better his mental, material and civil condition. Society is not corrupted from the apex but from the base. It is not the pure rain that falls from the heavens, but the stagnant waters of the pool, that breed disease and death. The corruption of the ballot by white men of the South is more pernicious than the misuse of it by black men; the perversion of the law in the apprehension and punishment of criminals, by being wielded almost exclusively against colored men, not only brings law into contempt of colored men but encourages crime among white men. Thus the entire society is corrupted. Mob law is the most forcible expression of an abnormal public opinion; it shows that society is rotten to the core. When men find that laws are purposely framed to oppress and defraud them they become desperate and reckless; and mob law, by usurping the rightful functions of the judiciary, makes criminals of honest men. As Alexander Pope expressed it:

> *Vice is a monster of such frightful mien,*
> *That to be hated needs but to be seen;*
> *Yet, seen too oft, familiar with his face,*
> *We first endure, then pity, then embrace.*

The South has nothing to gain and everything to lose in attempting to repress the energies and ambition of the colored man. It is to the safety as well as to the highest efficiency of society that all its members should be allowed the same opportunities for moral, intellectual and material development. "Do unto others as you would have them do unto you." "Thou shalt love thy neighbor as thyself." There is no escape from the law of God. You either deal justly or suffer the evil effects of wrong-doing. The disorders

which have made the South a seething cauldron for fifteen years
have produced the most widespread contempt of lawful authority not only on the part of the lawless whites but the law-abiding
blacks, who have suffered patiently the infliction of all manner
of wrong *because they were a generation of slaves, suddenly made
freemen.* They permitted themselves to be shot because they had
been educated to bare their backs at the command of the white
oligarch. But that sort of pusillanimous cowardice cannot be expected to last always. Men in a state of freedom instinctively
question the right of others to impose unequal burdens upon
them, or to deny to them equal and exact protection of the laws.
When oppressed people begin to murmur, grow restless and dis-
contented, the opposer had better change his tactics, or lock himself up, as does the cowardly tyrant of Russia.

A new generation of men has come upon the stage of action in
the South. They know little or nothing of the regulations or the
horrors of the slave régime. They know they are freemen; they
know they are cruelly and unjustly defrauded; and they *question
the right* of their equals to oppose and defraud them. A large
number of these people have enjoyed the advantage of common
school education, and not a few of academic and collegiate education, and a large number have "put money in their purse."
The entire race has so changed that they are almost a different people from what they were when the exigencies of war
made their manumission imperative. Yet there has been but little
change in the attitude of the white men towards this people. They
still strenuously deny their right to participate in the administration of justice or to share equally in the blessings of that justice.

There must be a change of policy. The progress of the black
man demands it; the interest of the white man compels it. The
South cannot hope to share in the industrious emigration constantly flowing into our ports as long as it is scattered over the
world that mob law and race distractions constantly interrupt the
industry of the people, and put life and property in jeopardy of

eminent disturbance; and she cannot hope to encourage the investment of large capital in the development of her industries or the extension of her national system. Capital is timid. It will only seek investment where it is sure of being let alone. Again, while the present state continues, no Southern statesman, however capable he may be, can hope to enjoy the confidence of the country or attain to high official position. Thoughtful, sober people will not entrust power to men who sanction mob law, and who rise to high honor by conniving at or participating in assassination and murder. They have too much self-respect to do it.

Only a few weeks since, a narrow-minded senator from the State of Alabama, speaking upon the question of "National Aid to Education," said he would rather vote for an appropriation to place the Southern States in direct communication with the Congo than to vote money to educate the blacks. There is no ingrate more execrable than the one who lifts up his hand or his voice to wrong the man he has betrayed. This senator from Alabama does not represent the majority of the people of his state. Take away the shot gun and mob law and he would be compelled to crawl back into the obscurity out of which he was dragged by his accomplices in roguery.

The colored man is in the South to stay there. He will not leave it voluntarily and he cannot be driven out. He had no voice in being carried into the South, but he will have a very loud voice in any attempt to put him out. The expatriation of 5,000,000 to 6,000,000 people to an alien country needs only to be suggested to create mirth and ridicule. The white men of the South had better make up their minds that the black men will remain in the South just as long as corn will tassel and cotton will bloom into whiteness. The talk about the black people being brought to this country to prepare themselves to evangelize Africa is so much religious nonsense boiled down to a sycophantic platitude. The Lord, who is eminently just, had no hand in their forcible coming here; it was preëminently the work of the devil. Africa will have to be evangelized *from within*, not *from without*. The Colonization society has spent mints of money and tons of human blood in the selfish attempt to plant an Anglo-African colony on the West Coast of Africa. The money has been thrown away and the human lives have been sacrificed in vain. The black people of this country are Americans, not Africans; and any wholesale expatriation of them is altogether out of the question.

The white men of the South should not deceive themselves: the blacks are with them to remain. Whether they like it or not, it is a fact that will not be rubbed out.

If this be true, what should be the policy of the whites towards the blacks? The question should need no answer at my hands. If it were not for the unexampled obtuseness of the editors, preachers and politicians of that section, I should close this chapter here.

The white men and women of the South should get down from the delectable mountain of delusive superiority which they have climbed; and, recognizing that "of one blood God made all the children of men," take hold of the missionary work God has placed under their nose.

Instead of railing at the black man, let them take hold of him in a Christian spirit and assist him in correcting those moral abscesses and that mental enervation which they did so awfully much to infuse into him; they should first take the elephant out of their own eyes before digging at the gnat in their neighbor's eyes. They should encourage him in his efforts at moral and religious improvement, not by standing off and clapping their hands, but by going into his churches and into his pulpits, showing him the "light and the way" not only by precept but example as well. Can't do it, do you say? Then take your religion and cast it to the dogs, for it is a living lie; it comes not from God but from Beelzebub the Prince of Darkness. A religion that divides Christians is unadulterated paganism; a minister that will not preach the Gospel to sinners, be they black or white, is a hypocrite, who "steals the livery of Heaven to serve the Devil in." They should make liberal provision for the schools set apart for the colored people, and they should visit these schools, not only to mark the progress made, and to encourage teacher and pupil, but to show to the young minds blossoming into maturity and usefulness that they are friends and deeply interested in the progress made. In public, they should seek first to inspire the confidence of colored men by just laws and friendly overtures and by encouraging the capable, honest and ambitious few by placing them in position of honor and trust. They should show to colored men that they accept the Constitution as amended, and are earnestly solicitous that they should prosper in the world, and become useful and respected citizens. You can't make a friend and partisan of a man by shooting him; you can't make a sober, industrious, honest man by robbing and outraging him. These tactics will not work to the uplifting of a people. "A soft answer turns away wrath." Even a dog caresses the hand that pats him on the head.

The South must spend less money on penitentiaries and more money on schools; she must use less powder and buckshot and more law and equity; she must pay less attention to politics and more attention to the development of her magnificent resources; she must get off the "race line" hobby and pay more attention to the common man; she must wake up to the fact that—

Worth makes the man, and want of it the fellow,

and that it is to her best interest to place all men upon the same footing before the law; mete out the same punishment to the white scamp that is inexorably meted out to the black scamp, for a scamp is a scamp any way you twist it; a social pest that should be put where he will be unable to harm any one. In an honest acceptance of the new conditions and responsibilities God has placed upon them, and in mutual forebearance, toleration and assistance, the South will find that panacea for which she has sought in vain down to this time.

CHAPTER XI

Land and Labor

There is more prose than poetry in the desperate conflict now waging in every part of the civilized world between labor and capital,—between the dog and his tail, again, for, when the question is reduced to a comprehensive statement of fact, it will be readily seen that capital is the offspring of labor, not labor the offspring of capital. Capital can produce nothing. Left to itself, it is as valueless as the countless millions of gold, silver, copper, lead and iron that lie buried in the unexplored womb of Nature. This storied wealth counts for nothing in its crude, undeveloped state. As it is to-day, so it was a thousand years ago. Years may add to the bulk, and, therefore, the richness of its value; but until man, by his labor of muscle and brain, has brought it forth, it has no value whatever. To have value, it must become an object of barter, of circulation, in short, of exchange. As its value depends upon its utility, so when it can no longer be used it again becomes a useless mass of perishable wealth. It is the product of labor, pure and simple. Speaking on "Management of the Banks" (footnote p. 223), in his work on *Labor and Capital*, Edward Kellogg says:—

All who become rich by speculations in bank, state and other stocks, gain their wealth at the expense of the producing classes; for no increased production is made by the changing market value of these stocks. It is clear, that when the rate of interest is increased, the gains of money-lenders are augmented, and the money gained will buy a greater quantity of property and labor. The increased gains of the lender must be paid by the borrowers, by the productions of their own or of *others'* labor.

So Adam Smith, speaking of "the Origin and Use of Money" (*Wealth of Nations,* p. 33), says:

> In order to avoid the inconveniency of such situations, every prudent man in every period of society, after the first establishment of the divisions of labor, must naturally have endeavored to manage his affairs in such a manner as to have at all times by him, besides the peculiar produce of his own industry, a certain quantity of some one commodity or other, such as he imagined few people would be likely to refuse in exchange for the produce of their industry.

Labor is the one paramount force which develops the resources of the world. It produces all the wealth; it pays, in the last analysis, all the taxes—National, State and municipal; it produces the wealth which sustains all the institutions of learning, as well as ministers to the profligate luxuries of the idlers and sharpers who add nothing to the wealth of society, but on the contrary constantly take from it, and who have not inaptly been termed by Dr. Howard Crosby the "dangerous classes;" it makes the wealth which gives a few men millions of dollars as their share, either as rental or usurious interest upon capital invested in the production of wealth; and it creates the vast surplus which lies in the coffers of the Federal and State treasuries of our land.

The producing agency, without which there could be no wealth; without which the landlord could exact no rent and capital could draw no interest, the producing agency alone receives an inadequate proportion of the wealth it produces. The man who conducts any business requiring labor and capital not only exacts an unjust proportion of the laborer's hire, but takes more than he justly should as interest upon his capital and as reward for his own time and labor, often amounting to no trouble or labor, he delegating to other hands, such as foremen or overseers, the absolute control of his investment. Yet, the man who invests capital not only derives, in a majority of cases, a sufficient income to enable him to live in more than comfort but to have a healthy bank account; while the laborer, who alone makes capital draw interest by giving it employment in developing the resources of nature, derives only a bare subsistence, frequently not sufficient to meet the absolute necessaries of his daily life. His wife and children must be content with life simply—bare, cold life—often without any of the conveniences or the commonest luxuries which make existence anything more than the curse it is to a large majority of humankind. This is peculiarly true of the condition of the masses of the Old World, and is fast becoming true in our own young and vigorous country.

In every quarter of the globe the cry of depressed and defrauded labor is heard. The enormous drain upon the producing agents necessary to maintain in idleness and luxury the great capitalists of the world who accumulated their ill-gotten wealth by fraud, perjury and "conquest," so called, grinds the producing agent down to the lowest possible point at which he can live and still produce. The millionaires of the world, so called "aristocracies," and the taxes imposed by sovereign states to liquidate obligations more frequently contracted to enslave than to ameliorate the conditions of mankind, are a constant drain which comes ultimately out of the laboring classes in every case.

What are millionaires, any way, but the most dangerous enemies of society, always eating away its entrails, like the cultures that preyed upon the chained Prometheus? Take our own breed of these parasites; note how they grind down the stipend they are compelled to bestow upon the human tools they must use to still further swell their ungodly gains! Note how they take advantage of the public; how they extort, with Shylock avarice, every penny they possibly can from those who are compelled to use the appliances which wealth enables them to contrive for the public convenience and comfort; how they corrupt legislatures and dictate to the unscrupulous minions of the law. The Athenians were wise who enacted into law the principle that when a citizen became too powerful or rich to be controlled within proper bounds, the safety of society demanded that he should be exiled—sent where his power or riches could not be used to the detriment of his fellow-citizens. Should such a rule be applied to-day, society in every land could disgorge with much advantage the men who ride the people as the Old Man of the Sea rode Sindbad the luckless sailor. But our civilization is built upon a higher conception of individual right and immunity; there is now no limit to the right of one man to rob another of the produce of his labor or his natural and conferred rights. Not only may individuals rob and plunder their fellows with absolute impunity, but our laws have put breath into that soulless thing which has become notoriously infamous as a "corporation." Around this thing, this engine of extortion and oppression, our laws have placed bulwarks which the defrauded laborer, the widow and orphan, and even the sovereign public, cannot overleap. Here is where Monopoly first shows its cormorant head.

If millionaires are enemies of society, and I assume that they are—not because they have property, but because, as a rule, they have acquired it by unjust processes and use it tyrannically—what excuse have we for aristocracies, an idle class, a privileged class, who toil not, nor spin? What is a recognized aristocracy, such as England maintains? From what perennial fountain did it draw its nobility and wealth? Came they not through Norman conquest and robbery? Who pay the heavy taxes levied upon the people to support the privileged classes of England? The royal revenues and princely preserves, are they not supported out of the sweat of the poorer classes, upon whom all the burdens of society fall at last? And why should there be royal revenues and princely preserves? Do they add anything to the wealth of a nation or the happiness of a people? Let us see.

Brassey (Sir Thomas), in his book on *Work and Wages*, p. 71, says:

The Irish Poor Law Commissioners stated that the average produce of the soil in Ireland was not much above one half the average produce in England, whilst the number of laborers employed in agriculture was, in proportion to the quantity of land under cultivation more than double, viz.: as five to two. Thus ten laborers in Ireland raised only the same quantity of produce that four laborers raised in England, and this produce was generally of an inferior quality.

Why is it that ten men in Ireland produce no more than four men produce in England?

Henry George says (*Social Problems*, p. 150) :

A year ago I traveled through that part of Ireland from which these government-aided emigrants come. What surprises an American at first, even in Connaught, is the apparent sparseness of population, and he wonders if this can indeed be that over-populated Ireland of which he has heard so much. *There is plenty of good land,* but on it are only fat beasts, and sheep so clean and white that you at first think that they must be washed and combed every morning. Once, this soil was tilled and was populous, but now you will find only traces of ruined hamlets, and here and there the miserable hut of a herd, who lives in a way that no Terra del Fuegan could envy. For the 'owners' of this land, who live in London and Paris, many of them having never seen their estates, find cattle more profitable than men, and so the men have been driven off. *It is only when you reach the bog and the rocks* in the mountains and by the sea shore, that you find a dense population. Here they are crowded together on land on which nature never intended men to live. It is too poor for grazing, so the people who have been driven from the better lands are allowed to live upon it—as long as they pay their rent. If it were not too pathetic, the patches they called fields would make you laugh. Originally the surface of the ground must have been about as susceptible of cultivation as the surface of Broadway. But at the cost of enormous labor the small stones have been picked off and piled up, though the great boulders remain, so that it is impossible to use a plow; and the surface of the bog has been cut away and manured by seaweed, brought in from the shore on the backs of men and women, till it can be made to grow something.

Sir Thomas Brassey writes from a capitalist's standpoint, while Mr. George writes from the standpoint of a philosopher who not only sees gross social wrongs but boldly applies the remedy. But let us see if the same fester which irritates the body of Irish society has not also a parasitical existence in our own land, where society is yet in its infancy, where the people are supposed to enjoy all the advantages of the competitive system, and where all are, measurably, free to take and to use the opportunities offered the pioneers, or him who gets first his grip upon the three natural elements absolutely essential to man's existence, viz.: air, water, and land.

Wm. Goodwin Moody says (*Land and Labor in the United States*, p. 77):

Instead of being able to boast, as could our fathers, that every man who tilled the soil was lord of the manor he occupied, owning no master, the last census report made a return of 1,024,701 tenant farms in our country in 1880.

A comparison of this showing with the land-holdings of Great Britain and Ireland will help to a better understanding of what these things import. The very latest statistics give the total number of holdings in England and Wales at 414,804; in Ireland, at 574,222; in Scotland, at 80,101; total, 1,069,127. Showing that in the whole of Great Britain and Ireland, counting all the holdings as tenant occupations, which they are not, there are 200,000 less tenant farms than in the United States.

Again:

Among the owners of the tenant farms in our country are English, French, and German capitalists, non-residents, who have bought immense tracts of the railroad lands, and seized upon the alternate government sections lying within their railroad purchases, and on those tracts have commenced their bonanza operations, or planted their tenants on the American system.

When it is remembered that the entire network of railroads in the United States is practically under the absolute control of five or six men who, having derived their valuable franchises and more than princely land grants from the people, show the utmost disregard of the comfort, convenience or rights of the donors; when it is remembered that one family in the city of New York controls enough land with enough tenants to constitute an overgrown village; and that what they do not claim as their own is held by one-fourth of the rest of the population; when it is remembered that nearly every article which has become a household necessity has been seized upon and can be obtained only through some corporation, in the manufacture of which the government has virtually granted a monopoly, as Charles granted to the Duke of Buckingham a monopoly in the sale of gold lace; when it is remembered that, even in this new country, three-fourths of the population rent their homes and cannot buy them*; when these things are remembered, as they should be, it will be readily seen that the condition of our work-people is fast becoming no better than that of the people of Europe, where a thousand years of false social adjustments, of usurpation and of tyranny, have reduced the proletariat class to the verge of starvation and desperation.

True, the immigrant laborers from Europe in the North, and the colored people at the South tend to crowd into the cities, where their labor is least needed and the conditions of life for them must be at the hardest; true, in America if a man *has it in him* the way is open for him to mount to the topmost round of the social ladder; true, too, the operatives in manufactures and the agricultural laborers here live on a far higher plane than in Europe; but the elements of degradation as well as of elevation are present in our land, and "easy in the descent" to the infernal regions. Let us be warned in time.

* W. G. Moody: *Land and Labor in the United States.*

CHAPTER XII

Civilization Degrades the Masses

There are men in all parts of the world, whose names have become synonyms of learning and genius, who proclaim it from the housetops that civilization is in a constant state of evolution to a higher, purer, nobler, happier condition of the people, the great mass of mankind, who properly make up society, and who have been styled, in derision, the *"mudsills* of society." So they are, society rests upon them; society must build upon them; without them society cannot be, because they are, in the broadest sense, society itself,—not only the "mudsills" but the *superstructure* as well. They not only constitute the great producing class but the great consuming class as well. They are the bone and sinew of society.

It is therefore of the utmost importance to know the condition of the people; it is not only important to know exactly what that condition is, but it is of the very first importance to the well-being of society that there should be absolutely nothing in that condition to arouse the apprehension of the sharks who live upon the carcass of the people, or of the people who permit the sharks to so live. There is nothing more absolutely certain than that the people—who submit to be robbed through the intricate and multifiarious processes devised by the cupidity of individuals and of governments—when aroused to a full sense of the wrongs inflicted upon them, will strike down their oppressors in a rage of desperation born of despair.

Modern tyrannies are far more insidious than the military despotisms of the past. These modern engines which crush society destroy the energy and vitality of the people by the slow process of starvation, sanctioned by the law, and in a majority of instances, are patiently borne by the victims. It is only when human nature can endure no more that protests are first heard; then armed resistance; then anarchy. Thus it was with the French of the eighteenth century. Thus it is with the Russian, the German, the English, the Irish peoples of to-day. The heel of the tyrant is studded with too many steel nails to be borne without excruciating pain and without earnest protest.

If in their desperate conflict with the serpent that has coiled its slimy length about the body of the people the latter resort to dynamite, and seek by savage warfare to right their wrongs, they are to be condemned and controlled, for they confound the innocent with the guilty and work ruin rather than reform. Yet there is another side to be considered, for when injustice wraps itself in the robes of virtue and of law, and calls in the assistance of armies and all the destructive machinery of modern warfare to enforce its right to enslave and starve mankind, what counter warfare can be too savage, too destructive in its operations, to compel attention to the wrong? The difficulty is that vengeance should discriminate, but that is a refinement which blind rage can hardly compass.

I believe in law and order; but I believe, as a condition precedent, that law and order should be predicated upon right and justice, pure and simple. Law is, intrinsically, a written expression of justice; if, on the contrary, it becomes instead written *injustice*, men are not, strictly speaking, bound to yield it obedience. There is no law, on the statute books of any nation of the world, which bears unjustly upon the people, which should be permitted to stand one hour. It is through the operations of law that mankind is ground to powder; it is by the prostitution of the rights of the masses, by men who pretend to be their representatives and are not, that misery, starvation and death fill the largest space in the news channels of every land.

In New York City—where the intelligence, the enterprise, the wealth and the christianized humanity of the New World are supposed to have their highest exemplification—men, women and children die by the thousands, starved and frozen out of the world! Thousands die yearly in the city of New York from the effects of exposure and insufficient nutriment. The world, into which they had come unbidden, and the fruits of which a just God had declared they should enjoy as reward of the sweat of their brows, had refused them even a bare subsistance; and, this, when millions of food rot in the storehouses without purchasers! The harpies of trade prefer that their substance should resolve itself into the dirt and weed from which it sprung, rather than the poor and needy should eat of it and live.

I have walked through the tenement wards of New York, and I have seen enough want and crime and blasted virtue to condemn the civilization which produced them and which fosters them in its bosom.

I have looked upon the vast army of police which New York City maintains to protect life and so-called "vested rights," and I have concluded that there is something wrong in the social system which can only be kept intact by the expenditure of so much productive force, for this vast army, which stands on the street corners and lurks in the alley ways, "spotting," suspicious persons, "keeping an eye" on strangers who look "smart," this vast army contributes nothing to the production of wealth. It is, essentially, a parasite. And yet, without this army of idlers, life would be in constant danger and property would fall prey not only to the vicious and the desperate, but to the hungry men and women who have neither a place to shelter them from the storms of heaven, nor food to sustain nature's cravings from finding an eternal resting place in the Potter's Field. And, even after every precaution which selfishness can devise, courts of law and police officers are powerless to stay the hand of the pariahs whom society has outlawed—the men and women who are doomed to starve to death and be buried at the expense of society. The streets of every city in the Union are full of people who have been made desperate by social adjustments which prophets laud to the skies and which philosophers commend as "ideal," as far as they go.

One-half the producing power of the United States is to-day absolutely dependent upon the cold charity of the world; one fourth does not make sufficient to live beyond the day, while the other one-fourth only manages to live comfortably at the expense of the most parsimonious economy.

It is becoming a mooted question whether labor-saving machinery has not supplanted muscle-power in the production of every article to such a marvelous extent as to make thoughtful men tremble for the future of those who can only hope to live upon the produce of their labors. The machine has taken the place, largely, of man in the production of articles of consumption, of wear and of ornamentation; but no machine has, as yet, been invented to take the place of human wants. The markets of the world are actually glutted with articles produced by machine labor, but there are no purchasers with the means to buy, to consume the additional production caused by machinery and the consequent cheapening of processes of producing the articles of consumption, ornamentation, etc. When men have work they have money; and when men have money they spend it. Hence, when the toilers of a land have steady employment trade is brisk; when business stagnation forces them into idleness vice and crime afflict the country.

What avail the tireless labor of the machine and the mountains of material it places upon the market, if there are no purchasers? One man at a machine will do as much work in a factory to-day as required the work of fifty men fifty years ago; but the enhanced volume of production can have only one purchaser now where there was once fifty, hence the fitful existence of the one and the desperate struggle for existence of the forty-nine.* As iron and steel cannot compete with muscle and brain in the volume of production, so iron and steel cannot compete with muscle and brain in consumption. And, without consumption, what does production amount to? What does it avail us that our stores and granaries are overstocked, if the people are unable to buy? The thing is reduced to a cruel mockery when stores and granaries are overgorged, while people clamor in vain for clothing and food, and drop dead within reach of these prime elements of warmth and sustentation.

What does it avail us if the balance of trade be in our favor by one, or two, or three hundred millions of dollars, if this result be obtained by the degradation and death of our own people? More; not only at the expense of the well being of our own people, but of the people of those countries in whose markets we are enabled to undersell them, by reason of the more systematic pauperization of our own producing classes.

Competition, it is declared, is the life of trade; if this be true, it is truer that it is the death of labor, of the poorer classes. For Great Britain has established herself in the markets of the world at the expense of her laboring classes. While the capitalists of that country hold up their heads among the proudest people of the world, her laboring classes are absolutely ground to powder. Because of the inhuman competition which her manufacturers have been led to adopt, and the introduction of improved labor-saving machinery, her balance of trade runs far into the millions of pounds, and political economists place their hands upon their hearts and declare that Great Britain is the most happy and prosperous country on the face of the globe. But the declaration is illusory in the extreme. No country can be happy and prosperous whose "mudsills" live in squalor, want, misery, vice and death.

* Wm. Goodwin Moody shows this conclusively in his work on *Land and Labor in the United States.*

If Great Britain is happy and prosperous, how shall we account for the constant strikes of labor organizations for higher pay or as a protest against further reduction of wages below which man cannot live and produce? The balance of trade desire is the curse of the people of the world. It can be obtained only by underbidding other people in their own markets; and this can be done only by the maximum of production at the minimum of cost—by forcing as much labor out of the man or the machine as possible at the least possible expense.

There is death in the theory; death to our own people and death to the people with whom we compete. When a people no longer produce those articles which are absolutely necessary to sustain life the days of such people may be easily calculated.

Men talk daily of "over production," of "glutted markets," and the like; but such is not a true statement of the case. There can be no over production of anything as long as there are hungry mouths to be fed. It does not matter if the possessors of these hungry mouths are too poor to buy the bread; if they are hungry, there is no overproduction. With a balance of $150,000,000 of trade; with plethoric granaries and elevators all over the land; with millions of swine, sheep and cattle on a thousand hills; with millions of surplus revenue in the vaults of the National treasury, diverted from the regular channels of trade by an ignorant set of legislators who have not gumption enough to reduce unnecessary and burdensome taxation without upsetting the industries of the country—with all its grandiloquent exhibition of happiness and prosperity, the laboring classes of the country starve to death, or eke out an existence still more horrible.

The factories of the land run on half time, and the men, women and children who operate them grow pinch-faced, lean and haggard, from insufficient nutriment, and are old and decrepit while yet in the bud of youth; the tenements are crowded to suffocation, breeding pestilence and death; while the wages paid to labor hardly serve to satisfy the exactions of the landlord—a monstrosity in the midst of civilization, whose very existence is a crying protest against our pretensions to civilization.

Yet, "competition" is the cry of the hour. Millionaires compete with each other in the management of vast railroads and water routes, reducing labor to the verge of subsistence while exacting mints of money as tolls for transportation from the toilers of the soil and the consumers who live by their labor in other industrial enterprises; the manufacturers join in the competition, selling goods at the least possible profit to themselves and the least possible profit to those who labor for them; and, when no market can be found at home, boldly enter foreign markets and successfully compete with manufacturers who employ what our writers are pleased to style "pauper" labor. Every branch of industry is in the field *competing*, and the competition is ruining every branch of industry. The constant effort to obtain the maximum of production at the minimum of cost operates injuriously upon employer and employee alike; while the shrinkage in money circulation, caused by the competition, reduces, in every branch of industry, the wages of those who are the great consumers as well as producers; it produces those "hard times" which bear so hardly upon the poor in every walk of life. Even the laboring man has entered the race, and now competes in the labor market with his fellow for an opportunity to make a crust of bread to feed his wife and child. When things reach this stage, when the man who is working for one dollar and a half per day is underbid by a man who will work for a dollar and a quarter, then the condition of the great wealth producing and consuming class is desperate indeed. And so it is.

Frederick Douglass, the great Negro commoner, speaking at Washington, April 16, 1883, on the "Twenty-first Anniversary of Emancipation in the District of Columbia," said:

Events are transpiring all around us that enforce respect of the oppressed classes. In one form or another, by one means or another, the ideas of a common humanity against privileged classes, of common rights against special privileges, are now rocking the world. Explosives are heard that rival the earthquake. They are causing despots to tremble, class rule to quail, thrones to shake and oppressive associated wealth to turn pale. It is for America to be wise in time.

And the black philosopher, who had by manly courage and matchless eloquence braved the mob law of the North and the organized brigandage and robbery of the South in the dark days of the past, days that tried men's souls, standing in the sunlight of rejuvenated manhood, still was the oracle of the oppressed in the sentiments above quoted.

All over the land the voice of the masses is heard. Organizations in their interests are multiplying like sands on the seashore. The fierce, hoarse mutter of the starved and starving gives unmistakable warning that America has entered upon that fierce conflict of money-power and muscle-power which now shake to their very centers the hoary-headed commonwealths of the old world. In *John Swinton's Paper* of a recent date I find the following editorial arraignment of the present state of "Labor and Capital:"

The cries of the people against the oppressions of capital and monopoly are heard all over the land; but the capitalist and monopolist give them no heed, and go on their way more relentlessly than ever. Congress is fully aware of the condition of things; but you cannot get any bill through there for the relief of the people. The coal lords of Pennsylvania know how abject are the tens of thousands of blackamoors of their mines; but they grind them without mercy, and cut their days' wages again whenever they squeal. Jay Gould knows of the wide-spread ruin he has wrought in piling up his hundred millions; but he drives along faster than ever in his routine of plunder. The factory Christians of Fall River see their thousands of poor spinners struggling for the bread of life amid the whirl of machinery: but they order reduction after reduction in the rate of wages, though the veins of the corporations are swollen to congestion. The "Big Four" of Chicago, who corner grain and provisions, and the capitalists here and elsewhere who do the same thing, know well how the farmers suffer and the tables of the poor are ravaged by their operations; but they prosecute their work more extensively and recklessly than ever. The railroad and telegraph corporations know that, in putting on "all that the traffic will bear," they are taking from this country more than the people can stand; yet their only answer is that of the horseleech. . . .

Our lawmakers know how the people are wronged through legislation in the interest of privilege and plunder; but they add statute to statute in that same interest. They know how advantageous to the producers would be the few measures asked in their name; yet they persistently refuse to adopt them. The great employers of labor, the cormorants of competition, know through what hideous injustice they enrich themselves; but speak to them of fair play, and they flout you from their presence. The wealthy corporations owning these street car lines in New York see that their drivers and conductors are kept on the rack from sixteen to eighteen hours every day of the week, including Sundays; but when a bill is brought into the State Legislature to limit the daily working hours to twelve, they order their hired agents of the lobby to defeat it. These gamblers of Wall street know that their gains are mainly through fraud; yet forever, fast and furious, do they play with loaded dice.

The landlords of these tenement quarters know by the mortality statistics how broad is the swathe that death cuts among their victims; but they add dollar to dollar as coffin after coffin is carried into the street. * * *

These owners of the machinery of industry know how it bears upon the men who keep it flying; but they are regardless of all that, if only it fills their coffers. These owners of palaces look upon the men by whom they are built; but think all the time how to raise the rent of their hovels. These great money-lenders who hold the mortgages on countless farms know of the straits of the mortgage-bound farmers; yet they never cease to plot for higher interest and harder terms. The gilded priests of Mammon and hypocrisy cannot get away from the cries of humankind; but when do you ever hear them denouncing the guilty and responsible criminals in their velvet-cushioned pews? Harder and harder grow the exactions of capital. Harder and harder grows the lot of the millions. Louder and louder grow the cries of the sufferers. Deafer and deafer grow the ears of the millionaires. *Yet*, if those who cry would but use their power in action, peaceful action, they could right their wrongs, or at least the most grievous of them, before the world completes the solar circuit of this year.

Wm. Goodwin Moody (*Land and Labor in the United States,* p. 338), reverting to the difficulties which beset the pathway of labor organizations, which have so far been productive of nothing but disaster to the laboring classes, says:

Is it not time that new weapons should be adopted, and new methods introduced? * * * Will not the working men of the country learn anything from the bitter experiences they have passed through, and abandon methods that have been so uniformly followed by the ultimate failure of all their efforts. But the great evils by which we are surrounded, and that are destroying the foundations of society, can be removed by the working-men only. They form the large majority of its members, and in our country they are all-powerful. Still it is only by absolutely united action that the working-men can accomplish any good. By disunion they may achieve any amount of evil. The enemy they have to contend against, though few in number, are strong in position and possession of great capital. Nevertheless, before the united working-men of the country, seeking really national objects and noble ends, by methods that are just and in harmony with the institutions under which we live, the tyranny of capital will end. The working-men will also draw to their support a very large part of the best thought and intelligence of the country, that will be sure to keep even step with the labor of society in its attack upon the enemies of humanity and progress.

There is no fact truer than this, that the accumulated wealth of the land, and the sources of power, are fast becoming concentrated in the hands of a few men, who use that wealth and power to the debasement and enthrallment of the wage workers. Already it is almost impossible to obtain any legislation, in State or Federal legislatures, to ameliorate the condition of the laboring classes. Capital has placed its tyrant grip upon the throat of the Goddess of Liberty. The power of railroad and telegraph corporations, and associated capital invested in monopolies which oppress the many, while ministering to the wealth, the comfort and the luxury of the few, has become omnipotent in halls of legislation, courts of justice, and even in the Executive Chambers of great States, so that the poor, the oppressed and the defrauded appeal in vain for justice.

Such is the deplorable condition of the laboring classes in the west, the north and the east. They are bound to the car of capital, and are being ground to powder as fast as day follows day. They organize in vain; they protest in vain; they appeal in vain. Civilization is doing its work. "To him that hath, more shall be given; to him that hath nothing, even that shall be taken from him."

Let us turn to the South and see if a black skin has anything to do with the tyranny of capital; let us see if the cause of the laboring man is not the same in all sections, in all States, in all governments, in the Union, as it is in all the world. If this can be shown; if I can incontestably demonstrate that *the condition of the black and the white laborer is the same, and that consequently*

CHAPTER XIII

Conditions of Labor in the South

⋆⎯⎯⎯◀◁◯◯◯▷▶⎯⎯⎯⋆

I am not seriously concerned about the frightful political disorders which have disgraced the Southern States since the close of the War of the Rebellion; nor am I seriously concerned about the race-wars in that section about which so much has been justly said, and about which so very little is really known, in spite of the vast mass of testimony that did not more than begin to tell the tale. I know that time and education will give proper adjustment to the politics of the South, and that the best men of all classes, the intelligent and the property-holders will eventually grasp the reins of political or civil power and give, as far as they can, equilibrium to the unbalanced conditions.

The men of natural parts, of superior culture and ambitious spirit usually, in all societies, manage to rise to the top as the natural rulers of the people. You cannot keep them down; you cannot repress them. They rise to the top as naturally as sparks fly upward to the heavens. Demagogues and quacks manage only to impose upon the ignorant and confiding, upon men, conscious of their own inability to rule, who gladly transfer the responsibility to the first loud-mouthed fellow who comes along claiming, as his own, superior capacity and virtue. Intelligent men do not permit ignoramuses and adventurers to rule them; they prefer to rule themselves; and they submit to be ruled by such interlopers only so long as it takes them to thoroughly understand the condition of affairs. It is not, therefore, to be marvelled at that the white men of the South spread death and terror in their pathway to the throne of power in subverting the governments of the Reconstruction policy, based as those governments were, upon *disorganized* ignorance on the part of the blacks and organized robbery on the part of the white adventurers, who have become infamous under the expressive term "carpet-baggers;" although the genuine Northern immigrants, the "Fools" who came in good faith to cast in their lot with the Southern people supposing themselves to be welcome, should not share in the obloquy of that epithet. But, should the white men of the South continue indefinitely as the rulers of the South, to the absolute exclusion af participation of the black citizens of those states, then would my surprise be turned into profound amazement and horror at what such tyranny would produce as a logical result. Yet I know the temper of the people of the South too well to base any deduction upon a proposition so full of horror and despair. And, then, too, such a proposition would be at variance with all accepted precedents of two peoples living in the same community, governed by the same laws and subject to the same social and material conditions. I submit that I have no fears about the future political status of the whites and blacks of the South. The intelligent, the ambitious and the wealthy men of *both races* will eventually rule over their less fortunate fellow-citizens without invidious regard to race or previous condition. And the great-grandson of Senator Wade Hampton may yet vote for the great-grandson of Congressman Robert Smalls to be Governor of the chivalric commonwealth of South Carolina. Senator Wade Hampton may grit his teeth at this aspect of the case; but it is strictly in the domain of probability. The grandson of John C. Calhoun, the great orator and statesman of South Carolina, has not as yet voted for a colored Governor, but he has for a colored sheriff and probate judge, as the following testimony he gave before the Blair committee on "Education and Labor," (Vol II, p. 173), in the city of New York, September 13, 1883, will show:

Q. (the Chairman) What do you think of his [the black man's] intellectual and moral qualities and his capacity for development? A. (Mr.
Calhoun, John C.) . . . The probate judge of my county is a Negro and one
of my tenants, and I am here now in New York attending to important business for my county as an appointee of that man. He has upon him the
responsibilities of all estates in the county; he is probate judge.

Q. Is he a capable man? A. A very capable man, and an excellent, good
man, and a very just one."

Again (*Ibid* p. 137), Mr. Calhoun testified:

The sheriff of my county is from Ohio, *and a Negro*, and he is a man whom
we all support in his office, because he is capable of administering his office.

When the grandson of John C. Calhoun can make such admissions, creditable alike to his head and his heart, may not the
great-grandson of Wade Hampton rise up to chase the Bourbon-
ism of his great-grandfather into the tomb of disgruntlement?
I have not the least doubt of such probability. Again, I say, I am
not seriously concerned about the future political status of the
black man of the South. He has talent; he has ambition; he possesses a rare fund of eloquence, of wit and of humor, and these
will carry him into the executive chambers of States, the halls of
legislation and on to the bench of the judiciary. You can't bar
him out; you can't repress him: he will make his way. God has
planted in his very nature those elements which constitute the
stock-in-trade of the American politician—ready eloquence, rich
humor, quick perception—and you may rest assured he will use
all of them to the very best advantage.

I know of municipalities in the South to-day, where capable
colored men are regularly voted into responsible positions by
the best white men of their cities. And why not? Do not colored
men vote white men into office? And, pray, is the white man less
magnanimous than the black man? Perish the thought! No; the
politics of the South will readily adjust themselves to the best
interest of the people; be very sure of this. And the future rulers
of the South will not all be white, nor will they be all black: they
will be a happy commingling of the two peoples.

And thus with the so-called "war of races:" it will pass away and leave not a trace behind. It is based upon condition and color-prejudice—two things which cannot perpetuate themselves. When the lowly condition of the black man has passed away; when he becomes a capable president of banks, of railroads and of steamboats; when he becomes a large land-holder, operating bonanza farms which enrich him and pauperize black and white labor; when he is not only a prisoner at the bar but a judge on the bench; when he sits in the halls of legislation the advocate of the people, or (more profit if less honor) the advocate of vast corporations and monopolies; when he has successfully metamorphosed the condition which attaches to him as a badge of slavery and degradation, and made a reputation for himself as a financier, statesman, advocate, land-holder, and money-shark generally, his color will be swallowed up in his reputation, his bank-account and his important money interests.

Is this a fancy picture? Is there no substantial truth seen in this picture of what will, must and shall be, as the logical outgrowth of the Divine affirmation that of one blood he created all men to dwell upon the earth, and of the Declaration of Independence that "we hold these truths to be self-evident:—That all men are created equal; that they are endowed by their Creator with certain unalienable rights; that among these are life, liberty and the pursuit of happiness"?

Let us see.

A few months ago I sat in the banking office of Mr. William E. Mathews and ex-Congressman Joseph H. Rainey (of South Carolina), in Washington. As I sat there, a stream of patrons came and went. The whites were largely in the majority. They all wanted to negotiate a loan, or to meet a note just matured. Among the men were contractors, merchants, department clerks, etc. They all spoke with the utmost deference to the colored gentleman who had money to loan upon good security and good interest.

A few months ago I dined with ex-Senator B. K. Bruce (of Mississippi), now Register of the United States Treasury. The ex-Senator has a handsome house, and a delightful family. In running my eyes over his card tray, I saw the names of some of the foremost men and women of the nation who had called upon Register and Mrs. Bruce. In passing through the Register's department with the Senator, sight-seeing, I was not surprised at the marks of respect shown to Mr. Bruce by the white ladies and gentlemen in his department. Why? Because Mr. Bruce is a gentleman by instinct, a diplomat by nature, and a scholar who has "burned the midnight oil." Such a person does not have to ask men and women to respect him; they do so instinctively.

I walked down F street and called at the office of Prof. Richard T. Greener, a ripe scholar and a gentleman. The professor not only has a paying law practice, but is president of a new insurance company. He has all that he can do, and his patrons are both black and white.

All this and more came under my observation in the course of an hour's leisure at the capital of the nation. And the black man has not yet aroused himself to a full sense of his responsibilities or of his opportunities.

In Baltimore, Philadelphia, New York, and Boston we have colored men of large wealth, who conduct extensive business operations and enjoy the confidence and esteem of their fellow citizens without regard to caste.

Speaking upon the progress of the colored race, in the course of an address on the "Civil Rights Law," at Washington, October 20, 1883, the Hon. John Mercer Langston, United States Minister and Consul General to Hayti, and one of the most remarkable, scholarly, and diplomatic men the colored race in America has produced, drew the following pen-picture:

Do you desire to witness moral wonders? Start at Chicago; travel to St. Louis; travel to Louisville; travel to Nashville; travel to Chattanooga; travel on to New Orleans, and in every State and city you will meet vast audiences, immense concourses of men and women with their children, boys and girls, who, degraded and in ignorance because of their slavery formerly, are to-day far advanced in general social improvement.

It would be remarkable now for you to go into the home of one of our families, and find even our daughters incompetent to discourse with you upon any subject of general interest with perfect ease and understanding. Excuse me, if I refer to the fact that some two weeks ago I visited St. Louis for two reasons; first to see my son and daughter, and secondly and mainly to attend the seventy-second anniversary of the birth of perhaps the richest colored man in the State of Missouri. I went to his house, and I was surprised as I entered his doors and looked about his sitting-room and parlors, furnished in the most approved modern style, in the richest manner; but I was more surprised when I saw one hundred guests come into the home of this venerable man, to celebrate the seventy-second anniversary of his birth, all beautifully attired; and when he told me, indirectly, how much money he had made, since the war, and what he was worth on the night of this celebration, I was more surprised than ever. I am surprised at the matchless progress the colored people of this country have made since their emancipation. I have traveled in the West Indies; I have seen the emancipated English, Spanish and French Negro; but I have seen no emancipated Negro anywhere who has made the progress at all comparable with the colored people of the United States of America.

I desire it to be distinctly understood, that I am not at all anxious about the mental and material development of the colored people of the United States. They are naturally shrewd, calculating and agreeable, possessing in a peculiar degree the art of pleasing; and these qualities will give them creditable positions in the business interests of the country in a few years. But they must have time to collect their wits, to sharpen their intelligence, to train their moral sense and the feeling of social responsibility, to fully comprehend all that the change from chattel slavery to absolute freedom implies. Men cannot awaken from a Rip Van Winkle slumber of a hundred years and grasp at once the altered conditions which flash upon them. The awakening is terrific, appalling, staggering.

When a man has been confined for long years in a dark dungeon he has not trouble in discerning objects about him which, when he first entered his dungeon, were indistinct or invisible to him. So when he is brought suddenly to the strong light of the sun the effulgence overmasters him, and he is blind as a bat. But slowly and painfully he becomes accustomed to the transition from absolute darkness to absolute light, and then nature wears to his vision her naturally gay and winsome appearance. So with the slave. His grasp of the conditions of freedom is slow and uncertain. But give him time, lend him a helping hand, and he will completely master the situation.

In one of the most remarkable pamphlets of the time, written by C. K. Marshall, D. D., of Vicksburg, Miss., entitled *The Colored Race Weighed in the Balance,* being a reply to a most malicious speech by J. L. Tucker, D. D., of Jackson, Miss., I find many truths that the American people should know. Both Dr. Marshall and Dr. Tucker are white ministers of the South, and both should be intimately acquainted with the characteristics, capacity and progress of the colored people. But Dr. Tucker appears to be as ignorant of the colored race as if he had spent his days in the Sandwich Islands instead of the sunny land of the South.

Dr. Marshall says (p. 55):

I think I know nearly all that can be said against a Negro. In one form or another, the complaints have been a thousand times reiterated; but has he not been, and is he not now what the white man and society have made him? He is naturally peace-loving, docile, and imitative. If kindly and justly treated, with due allowance for the *peculiar elements* that make up his life, he will render back, in kind at least, equally with the brother in white in *like surroundings.* Everybody knows some reliable, trustworthy Negro man and woman; and John Randolph said that of two of the politest men he ever saw one was a Negro. *Gentleness* is a wonderful agency in managing a Negro: I know it tells powerfully upon white folks. The psalmist, addressing his Maker, says, "Thy gentleness hath made me great." It is a mighty lever; it moves the world; it moved it before Archimedes; it moves it still; but peevishness, faultfinding, scolding, cursing, premature censure, haughty and assuming ways, sullenness, ill-temper, whether in the field, the kitchen, the nursery, or parlor, will legitimately result in thriftlessness, revolt, departure, and contempt for white people! Many of the young generation have not yet found their places in the new order of things; and their silly parents work themselves nearly to death to keep their sons from the plow and to make ladies of their daughters, just like white folks; but time, gentleness, bread, and neat homes will, with religion and culture, bring great changes. And I say it to the credit of their former owners, and their own instincts and capabilities, that *they constitute to-day the best peasantry, holding similar relations to the ruling classes on the face of the earth.* Their vices are no greater; their respect for law about the same; and their care for their children little inferior. Besides, they speak the language of their country better, are less cringing and craven, freer from begging; more manly, more polite, less priest-ridden, less obsequious; have a higher estimate of human rights and obligations; understand farming, cooking, house-work, and manual labor, in which they have been trained, better, I insist, than any similarly conditioned race or people. They are less profane—very much less—than white people; less bitter, vindictive, and bloodthirsty; less intemperate, and far, far less revengeful; and less selfish than what they contemptuously snub as "poor white trash." But he is a sinner! I believe the old stale rhyme tells some truth in a modified sense, "In Adam's fall we sinned all;" but I do not believe the serpent's tooth struck a more deadly and depraving virus into the Negro's share of the apple of Eden, dooming him as a sinner to a lower plane of wickedness than others. He commits not all, but many, of the sins, crimes, and misdemeanors, and indulges many of the vices of polished humanity—cultured Caucasian humanity. They have had but moderate experience in the sole management of their own affairs.

Again (p. 66):

The Negro is neither a beggar, nor a pauper, nor a tramp; and if honestly dealt with, he can make his own way. Where they are idle and profligate, execute the law vigorously against them, and they will approve and aid in the work. We can lift them up, or cast them down. For one, I think we owe them a debt of gratitude and impartial justice for their faithful conduct during the war; and when disposed to criticise and reproach them for not coming in all things up to your sentimental notions, just put yourself in their place. Then you will, if your scales are true and your weights just, settle the question with little difficulty. I cannot serve my readers better, perhaps, than by quoting the words of the Rev. Dr. Callaway, lately Professor in Emory College, Oxford, Ga., and new President of Paine Institute, Augusta, Ga., a native of that State, and to the manor born. In a late address, he says: "We have spoken of the Negro as related to the conduct of the war, but it remains to be said that, in his relation to us as a friend during that period, and to our wives and children as guardian, the testimony of his fidelity is on the lips of every surviving soldier. It is easy to conjecture how, with a race less loyal to home and patron, the testimony in the case might have been a narrative of lawlessness and license. What he refrained from, therefore, is to his credit. But in the four years of darkness and demoralization, when, besides those of military age, every boy whose muscles were equal to the support of a musket, and every old man with vigor enough to mark time, was called to the front, the Negro, commanding as a patriarch and reverent as a priest, kept sacred vigil at our homes. Besides this, with a foresight not developed for himself or his family, but evoked by virtue of his office, and the piteous destitution of our loved ones, he provided for their wants. 'They were a-hungered, and he fed them.' What he did is to his honor. What we refrain from in our place of power as the superior race, shall be to our credit; what we do in return shall be in proof of our appreciation. The conduct of the Negro during the war proves him kindly, temperate, trustworthy; his conduct since the war reveals in him considerateness, purpose, capacity, an order of growing good qualities. During the war his inferior courage, it may be assumed, inured to his superior serviceableness, his fears giving counsel to his courtesy and care. So set it down, if you will, though the logic is as lame as the charge is ungrateful."

This testimony upon the character, temper and adaptability of colored people is all the more valuable because Dr. Marshall not only treats the question from a Christian standpoint, but because his intimate acquaintance with the subject adds weight and authority to his opinion.

In the same strain, Dr. Atticus G. Haygood, President of Emory College, in Georgia, a man of the largest culture, Christian intelligence and progressive ideas, says, in his masterful work, *Our Brother in Black, His Freedom and His Future* (p. 194):

If white people and black people wish to know how to treat each other in all the relations of life, let them study the Bible. Take for example the business relations of life, the old question of capital and labor, of service and wages. For the settlement of all questions that grow out of these relations the laws laid down and the principles taught in the Bible, are worth all the "political economies" in the world. They apply to all races and conditions of men, in all countries and in all times. They are as needful and useful in New England factories as on Southern plantations. Free Negroes are not the only underlings in the world, Negro servants are not the only hirelings. There are thousands of factory operatives, day laborers, domestic servants, mechanics, sewing women, clerks, apprentices, and such like, whose cry for justice against oppression goes up to heaven by day and by night. "For which things' sake," in all lands, "the wrath of God is come upon the children of disobedience." Let us here recall some of these half-forgotten laws; they must do us all good. I know they are needed in the South; I am persuaded that they are needed wherever there are masters and servants.

Having heard a great deal about the condition of the colored people in Louisiana, I decided that it would not be uninteresting to have an authentic statement of that condition by some person fully capable of furnishing the desired information. I therefore addressed a letter to the Hon. Theophile T. Allain, a colored member of the Louisiana Legislature for Sweet Iberville parish, and a large sugar planter. From Mr. Allain's letter I condense the following statement, which will be found to be interesting for many reasons:

"First," says Mr. Allain, "I speak as a man of the South, who pays taxes on thirty-five thousand dollars worth of property, and without owing to any man one dollar. I claim to be well informed as to the condition of the colored people of the South, the people who bear the heat and burden of the day.

"In the cotton section of the South the Negroes are kept in subjugation, and are not permitted to exercise the right of suffrage guaranteed to them by the provisions of the Federal constitution. In the sugar-growing districts of Louisiana the colored and white people live upon terms of friendship and cordiality. In these districts there are thousands of colored men, who before the war were slaves, who now pay taxes upon property, assessed in their own names, ranging in value from five hundred to fifty thousand dollars. They produce principally rice and sugar. It is a self-evident fact that the labor of the colored men produces two-thirds of all the cotton raised in the South, four-fifths of the sugar, and nine-tenths of all the rice.

"In the cotton sections of Louisiana the colored men work mostly on shares, and here and there some of them have accumulated a little money; but, as a rule, they make fortunes for the landlords and die in poverty because of no fault of their own. Rent here, as everywhere else, pulls the laborer down, and keeps him down. What remains to him after the landlord has taken his *share*, goes to the Jew shopkeepers and other midle men at crossroads, who will not be satisfied with any profit less than one hundred to one hundred and fifty per cent.

"But the sugar districts of Louisiana are like oases in the desert. Vacuum pans, steam cars, fine machinery and smiling faces are to be met on every hand. Colored laborers find employment very readily in the sugar districts from October to February; and during cultivation-time, in many places, the colored laborers receive *as high as one dollar and twenty cents per day*, and during the grinding season, which is the harvest time, laborers receive from one dollar and twenty-five cents to one dollar and fifty cents per day in the field and seventy-five cents for one half of the night. At this season we run the sugar machinery night and day. I should not omit to state that colored men are, in the majority of cases, employed as engineers at our sugar mills, and receive from two to two and a half dollars per day:

"You will be surprised when I tell you that the most of the bricklaying and plastering work, and the blacksmithing and carpentering work is done in the sugar districts by colored men, who average three dollars per day for their work.

"There are fifty-eight parishes in Louisiana, twenty-four of them being sugar districts. To illustrate the degree of toleration which obtains in the cotton and sugar growing districts, take the following statement: In the Louisiana House of Representatives there are thirteen colored members—all from the sugar districts; in the Senate there are four colored members—all from the sugar districts. This condition of things is readily accounted for by the fact that the colored people in the sugar districts are more generally tax payers than they are in the cotton districts, and, having mutual interests, both white and black are more tolerant and better informed. The Bulldozer and White Liner can find but little room to ply their nefarious work where everybody finds plenty of work that pays well, and where material prosperity is the first and political bickering the secondary consideration. Because of the mutual interests at stake, colored men in the sugar districts are often protected by their bitterest political opponents.

"The State of Louisiana is assessed at $200,000,000, of which her colored population pay taxes upon more than $30,000,000. —Two thirds of this is owned by colored men in the sugar districts."

I could multiply quotations, but they would serve only to confirm my view, that the colored man merely requires time to fully comprehend his freedom and his opportunities, to enjoy the ample immunities of the first and to improve to the utmost the advantages of the second. All over the country the colored man is coming to understand that if he is ever to have and enjoy a status in this country at all commensurate with that of his white fellow-citizens, he must get his grip upon the elements of success which they employ with such effect, and boldly enter the lists, a competitor who must make a way for himself. Dr. Marshall says truly: "The Negro is neither a beggar, nor a pauper, nor a tramp." He is, essentially, a man of the largest wealth, God having given him, under tropical conditions, a powerful physique, with ample muscle and constitution to extract out of the repositories of nature her buried wealth. He only needs intelligence to use the wealth he creates. When he has intelligence, he will no longer labor to enrich men more designing and unscrupulous than he is; he will labor to enrich himself and his children. Indeed, in his powerful muscle and enduring physical constitution, directed by intelligence, the black man of the South, who alone has demonstrated his capacity to labor with success in the rice swamps, the cotton, and the cornfields of the South, will ultimately turn the tables upon the unscrupulous harpies who have robbed him for more than two hundred years; and from having been the slave of these men, he, in turn, will enslave them. From having been the slave, he will become the master; from having labored to enrich others, he will force others to labor to enrich him. The laws of nature are inexorable, and this is one of them.

The white men of the South may turn pale with rage at this aspect of the case, but it is written on the wall. Already I have seen in the South the black and white farm laborer, working side by side for a black landlord; already I have seen in the South a black and a white brick-mason (and carpenters as well) working upon a building side by side, under a colored contractor. And we are not yet two decades from the surrender of Robert E. Lee and the manumission of the black slave.

I have no disposition to infuriate any white man of the South, by placing a red flag before him; we simply desire to accustom him to look upon a picture which his grand-children will not, because of the frequency of the occurrence, regard with anything more heart-rending than complacent indifference. The world moves forward; and the white man of the South could not stand still, if he so desired. Like the black man, he must work, or perish; like the black man, he must submit to the sharpest competition, and rise or fall, as the case may be. And so it should be.

CHAPTER XIV

Classes in the South

Since the war the people of the South are, from a Northern standpoint, very poor. There are very few millionaires among them. A man who has a bank account of fifty thousand dollars is regarded as very rich. I am reminded of an incident which shows that the Southern people fall down and worship a golden calf the same as their deluded brothers of the North and West.

A few years ago I was a resident of Jacksonville, the metropolis of Florida. Florida is a great Winter resort. The wealthy people of the country go there for a few months or weeks in the Winter. It is fashionable to do so. A great many wealthy northern men have acquired valuable landed interests in Jacksonville, among them the Astors of New York, who have a knack for pinning their interests in the soil. The people of Jacksonville were very proud to have as a resident and property holder, Mr. Wm. B. Astor. And Mr. Astor appeared to enjoy immensely the worship bestowed upon his money. He built one or two very fine buildings there, which must net him a handsome return for his investment by this time. Mr. Astor had with him a very shrewd "Man Friday," and this Man Friday got it into his head that he would like to be Mayor of Jacksonville, and he sought and obtained the support of his very powerful patron. It leaked out that Mr. Astor favored his Man Friday for Mayor. The "business interests" of the city took the matter "under advisement." After much "consultation" and preliminary skirmishing, it was decided that it would be unwise to antagonize Mr. Astor's Man Friday; and so he was placed in nomination as the "Citizens' Candidate." He was elected by a handsome majority. I believe it is a disputed question to-day, whether Mr. Astor's Man Friday was, or was not, a citizen of the place at the time he was elected Mayor. Be that as it may, it showed beyond question that the people knew how to go down upon their knees to the golden calf.

A condition of slavery or of serfdom produces two grievous evils, around which cluster many others of less importance, viz: the creation of vast landed estates, and the pauperization and debasement of labor. Pliny declared that to the creation of vast *latifundia* (aggregated estates) Italy owed its downfall. The same is true of the downfall of the South and its pet institution, since they produced a powerful and arrogant class which was not content to lord it on their vast demesnes and over their pauper labor, but must needs carry their high-flown notions into the councils of the nation, flaunting their gentle birth and undulating acres in the faces of horny-handed statesmen like Abraham Lincoln, Henry Wilson, and others.

The operations of the vast landed estates of the South produced all the industrial disjointments which have afflicted the South since the war. The white man was taught to look upon labor as the natural portion of the black slave; and nothing could induce a white man to put his hand to the plow, but the gaunt visage of starvation at his door. He even preferred ignominious starvation to honest work; and, in his desperate struggle to avoid the horror of the one and the disgrace of the other, he would sink himself lower in the scale of moral infamy than the black slave he despised. He would make of himself a monster of cruelty or of abject servility to avoid starvation or honest work. It was from this class of vermin that the planters secured their "Nigger drivers" or overseers, and a more pliable, servile, cruel, heartless set of men never existed. They were commonly known as "*poor white trash*," or "crackers." They were most heartily and righteously detested by the slave population. As the poor whites of the South were fifty years ago, so they are to-day—a careless, ignorant, lazy, but withal, arrogant set, who add nothing to the productive wealth of the community because they are too lazy to work, and who take nothing from that wealth because they are too poor to purchase. They have graded human wants to a point below which man could not go without starving. They live upon the poorest land in the South, the "piney woods," and raise a few potatoes and corn, and a few pigs, which never grow to be hogs, so sterile is the land upon which they are turned to "root, or die." These characteristic pigs are derisively called "shotes" by those who have seen their lean, lank and hungry development. They are awful counterparts of their pauper owners. It may be taken as an index of the quality of the soil and the condition of the people, to observe the condition of their live stock. Strange as it may appear, the faithful dog is the only animal which appears to thrive on "piney woods" land. The "piney woods" gopher, which may be not inappropriately termed a "highland turtle," is a great desideratum in the food supply of the pauper denizens of these portions of the South. There is nothing enticing about the appearance of the gopher. But his flesh, properly cooked, is passably palatable.

The poor white population of the South who live in the piney woods are sunk in the lowest ignorance, and practice vices too heinous to be breathed. They have no schools, and their mental condition hardly warrants the charitable inference that they would profit much if they were supplied with them. Still, I would like to see the experiment tried. Their horrible poverty, their appalling illiteracy, their deplorable moral enervation, deserve the pity of mankind and the assistance of philanthropic men and a thoughtful government. Though sunk to the lowest moral scale, *they are men,* and nothing should be omitted to improve their condition and make them more useful members of the communities in which they are now more than an incubus.

It may not be out of place here to state that the Kuklux Klan, the White Liners League, the Knights of the White Camelia, and other lawless gangs which have in the past fifteen years made Southern chivalry a by-word and reproach among the nations of the earth, were largely recruited from this idle, vicious, ignorant class of Southerners. They needed no preparation for the bloody work perpetrated by those lawless organizations, those more cruel than Italian brigands. They instinctively hate the black man; because the condition of the black, his superior capacity for labor and receptivity of useful knowledge, place him a few pegs higher than themselves in the social scale. So these degraded white men, the very substratum of Southern population, were ready tools in the hands of the organized chivalrous brigands (as they had been of the slave oligarch), whose superior intelligence made them blush at the lawlessness they inspired, and who, therefore, gladly transferred to other hands the execution of those deeds of blood and death which make men shudder even now to think of them. It was long a common saying among the black population of the South that "I'd rudder be a niggah den a po' w'ite man!" and they were wise in their preference.

It is safe to say, that the peasantry of no country claiming to be civilized stands more in need of the labors of the schoolmaster and the preacher, than do the so-called "poor white trash" of the South. On their account, if no other, I am an advocate of a compulsory system of education, a National Board of Education, and a very large National appropriation for common school and industrial education.

I name this class first because it is the very lowest.

Next to this class is the great labor force of the South, the class upon whose ample shoulders have fallen the weight of Southern labor and inhumanity for lo! two hundred years—*the black man.* Time was, yesterday, it appears to me, when this great class were all of *one* condition, driven from the rising to the setting of the sun to enrich men who were created out of the same sod, and in the

construction of whose mysterious mechanism, mental and physical, the great God expended no more time or ingenuity. Up to
the close of the Rebellion, of that gigantic conflict which shook
the pillars of republican government to their center, the great
black population were truly the "mudsills" of Southern society,
upon which rested all the industrial burdens of that section; truly,
"the hewers of wood and the drawers of water;" a people who, in
the mysterious providence of God, were torn root and branch
from their savage homes in that land which has now become to
them a dream "more insubstantial than a pageant faded," to
"dwell in a strange land, among strangers," to endure, like the
children of Israel, a season of cruel probation, and then to begin
life in earnest; to put their shoulders to the wheel and assist in
making this vast continent, this asylum of the oppressed of the
world, the grandest abode of mingled happiness and woe, and
wealth and pauperization ever reared by the genius and governed
by the selfishness and cupidity of man. And to-day, as in the dark
days of the past, this people are the bone and sinew of the South,
the great producers and partial consumers of her wealth; the despised, yet indispensable, "mudsills" of her industrial interests.

A Senator of the United States from the South, whose hands
have been dyed in the blood of his fellow citizens, and who holds
his high office by fraud and usurpation, not long since declared
that his State could very well dispense with her black population.
That population outnumbers the white three to one; and by the
toil by which that State has been enriched, by the blood and the
sweat of two hundred years which the soil of that State has absorbed, by the present production and consumption of wealth by
that black population, we are amazed at the ignorance of the great
man who has been placed in a "little brief authority." The black
population cannot and will not be dispensed with; because it is so
deeply rooted in the soil that it is a part of it—the most valuable
part. And the time will come when it will hold its title to the land,
by right of purchase, for a laborer is worthy of his hire, and is

now free to invest that hire as it pleases him best. Already some of the very best soil of that State is held by the people this great magnus in the Nation's councils would supersede in their divine rights.

When the war closed, as I said, the great black population of the South was distinctively a laboring class. It owned no lands, houses, banks, stores, or live stock, or other wealth. Not only was it the distinctively laboring class but the distinctively pauper class. It had neither money, intelligence nor morals with which to begin the hard struggle of life. It was absolutely at the bottom of the social ladder. It possessed nothing but health and muscle.

I have frequently contemplated with profound amazement the momentous mass of subjected human force, a force which had been educated by the lash and the bloodhound to despise labor, which was thrown upon itself by the wording of the Emancipation Proclamation and the surrender of Robert E. Lee. Nothing in the history of mankind is at all comparable, an exact counterpart, in all particulars, to that great event. A slavery of two hundred years had dwarfed the intelligence and morality of this people, and made them to look upon labor as the most baneful of all the curses a just God can inflict upon humankind; and they were turned loose upon the land, without a dollar in their hands, and, like the great Christ and the fowls of the air, without a place to lay their head.

And yet to-day, this people, who, only a few years ago, were bankrupts in morality, in intelligence, and in wealth, have leaped forward in the battle of progress like *veterans*; have built magnificent churches, with a membership of over two million souls; have preachers, learned and eloquent; have professors in colleges by the hundreds and schoolmasters by the thousands; have accumulated large landed interests in country, town and city; have established banking houses and railroads; manage large coal, grocery and merchant tailoring businesses; conduct with ability and success large and influential newspaper enterprises; in short, have come, and that very rapidly, into sharp competition with white men (who have the prestige of a thousand years of civilization and opportunity) in all the industrial interests which make a people great, respected and feared. The metamorphosis has been rapid, marvelous, astounding. Their home life has been largely transformed into the quality of purity and refinement which should characterize the home; they have now successful farmers, merchants, ministers, lawyers, editors, educators, physicians, legislators—in short, they have entered every avenue of industry and thought. Their efforts yet crude and their grasp uncertain, but they are in the field of competition, and will remain there and acquit themselves manfully.

Of course I speak in general terms of the progress the colored people have made. Individual effort and success are the indicators of the vitality and genius of a people. When individuals rise out of the indistinguishable mass and make their mark, we may rest assured that the mass is rich and capable of unlimited production. The great mass of every government, of every people, while adding to and creating greatness, go down in history unmentioned. But their glory, their genius, success and happiness, are expended and survive in the few great spirits their fortunate condition produced. The governments of antiquity were great and glorious, because their proletarians were intelligent, thrifty and brave, but the proletarians fade into vagueness, and are great only in the few great names which have been handed down to us. It has been said that a nation expends a hundred years of its vitality in the production of a great man of genius like Socrates, or Bacon, or Toussaint l'Overture, or Fulton. And this may be true. There can now be no question that the African race in the United States possess every element of vitality and genius possessed by their fellow citizens of other races, and any calculation of race possibilities in this country which assumes that they will remain indefinitely the "mudsills" only of society will prove more brittle than ropes of sand.

At this time the colored people of the South are largely the industrial class; that is, they are the producing class. They are principally the agriculturists of the South; consequently, being wedded to the soil by life-long association and interest, and being principally the laboring class, they will naturally invest their surplus earnings in the purchase of the soil. Herein lies the great hope of the future. For the man who owns the soil largely owns and dictates to the men who are compelled to live upon it and derive their subsistence from it. The colored people of the South recognize this fact. And if there is any one idiosyncrasy more marked than another among them, it is their mania for buying land. They all live and labor in the cheerful anticipation of some day owning a home, a farm of their own. As the race grows in intelligence this mania for land owning becomes more and more pronounced. At first their impecuniosity will compel them to purchase poor hill-lands, but they will eventually get their grip upon the rich alluvial lands.

The class next to the great black class is the *small white farmers*. This class is composed of some of the "best families" of the South who were thrown upon their resources of brain and muscle by the results of the war, and of some of the worst families drawn from the more thrifty poor white class. Southern political economists labor hard to make it appear that the vastly increased production of wealth in the South since the war is to be traced largely to the phenomenally increased percentum of small white farmers, but the assumption is too transparent to impose upon any save those most ignorant of the industrial conditions of the South, and the marvelous adaptability to the new conditions shown by colored men. I grant that these small white farmers, who were almost too inconsiderable in numbers to be taken into account before the war, have added largely to the development of the country and the production of wealth; but that the tremendous gains of free labor as against slave labor are to be placed principally to their intelligence and industry is too absurd to be seriously debated.

The Charleston (S.C.) *News and Courier*, a pronounced anti-negro newspaper, recently made such a charge in all seriousness. The struggle for supremacy will largely come between the small white and black farmer; because each recurring year will augment the number of each class of small holders. A condition of freedom and open competition makes the fight equal, in many respects. Which will prove the more successful small holder, the black or the white?

The fourth class is composed of the *hereditary land-lords* of the South; the gentlemen with flowing locks, gentle blood and irascible tempers, who appeal to the code of honor (in times past) to settle small differences with their equals and shoot down their inferiors without premeditation or compunction, and who drown their sorrows, as well as their joviality in rye or Bourbon whiskey; the gentlemen who claim consanguinity with Europe's titled sharks, and vaunt their chivalry in contrast to the peasant or yeoman blood of all other Americans; the gentlemen who got their broad acres (however they came by their peculiar blood) by robbing black men, women and children of the produce of their toil under the system of slavery, and who maintain themselves in their reduced condition by driving hard bargains with white and black labor either as planters or shop-keepers, often as both, the dual occupations more effectually enabling them to make unreasonable contracts and exactions of those they live to victimize. They are the gentlemen who constantly declare that "this is a white man's government," and that "the Negro must be made to keep his place." They are the gentlemen who have their grip upon the throat of Southern labor; who hold vast areas of land, the product of robbery, for a rise in values; who run the stores and torture the small farmer to death by usurious charges for necessaries; these are the gentlemen who are opposed to the new conditions resultant from the war which their Hotspur impetuosity and Shylock greed made possible. In short, these gentlemen comprise the moneyed class. They are the gentlemen who are hastening the conflict of labor and capital in the South. And, when the black laborer and the white laborer come to their senses, join issues with the common enemy and pitch the tent of battle, then will come the tug of war.

But the large land-owners and tradesmen of the South will not in the future belong exclusively to the class of persons I have described. On the contrary this class of hereditary land-owners will be sensibly diminished and their places be taken by successful recruits from the ranks of small white and black farmers. Indeed, I confess, I strongly incline to the belief that the black man of the South will eventually become the large land-holding class, and, therefore, the future tyrants of labor in that section. All the indications strongly point to such a possibility. It is estimated that, already, the colored people own, in the cotton growing states, 2,680,800 acres, the result of seventeen years of thrift, economy, and judicious management; while in the State of Georgia alone they own, it is reliably estimated, 680,000 acres of land, and pay taxes on $9,000,000 worth of property. Dr. Alexander Crummell, a most learned African, in a very interesting pamphlet drawn out by the malicious misstatements of Dr. Tucker, before referred to by me, makes the following deductions and statements, to wit:

Let me suggest here another estimate of this landed property of the Negro, acquired *since* emancipation. Taking the old slave States in the general, there has been a large acquisition of land in each and all of them. In the State of Georgia, as we have just seen, it was 680,000 acres. Let us put the figure as low as 400,000 for each State—for the purchase of farm lands has been everywhere a passion with the freedman—this 400,000 acres multiplied into 14, *i. e.* the number of the chief Southern States, shows an aggregate of 5,600,000 acres of land, the acquisition of the black race in less than twenty years.

But Dr. Tucker will observe a further fact of magnitude in this connection: It is the increased PRODUCTION which has been developed on the part of the freedman since emancipation. I present but *one* staple, and for the reason that it is almost exclusively the result of FREE NEGRO LABOR.

I will take the five years immediately preceding the late civil war and compare them with the five years preceeding the last year's census-taking;

and the contrast in the number of cotton-bales produced will show the industry
and thrift of the black race as a consequent on the gift of freedom:

Years	Bales
1857	2,939,519
1858	3,113,962
1859	3,851,481
1860	4,669,770
1861	3,656,006
Total	18,230,738

Years	Bales
1878	4,811,265
1879	5,073,531
1880	5,757,397
1881	6,589,329
1882	5,435,845
The five years' work of *freedom*	27,667,367
The five years' work of *slavery*	18,230,738
Balance in favor of freedom	9,436,629

Now this item of production is a positive disproof of Dr. Tucker's statement, "that the average level in material prosperity is but little higher than it
was before the war." Here is the fact that the Freedman has produced one-
third more in five years than he did in the same time when a slave!

Another view of this matter is still more striking. The excess of yield in
cotton in seven years [*i.e.*, from 1875 to 1882] over the seven years [*i.e.*, from
1854 to 1861] is 17,091,000 bales, being AN AVERAGE ANNUAL INCREASE OF
1,000,000 BALES. If Dr. Tucker will glance at the great increase of the cotton,
tobacco, and sugar crops South, as shown in Agricultural Reports from 1865
to 1882, and reflect that NEGROES have been the producers of these crops, he
will understand their indignation at his outrageous charges of "laziness and
vagabondage:" and perhaps he will listen to their demand that he shall take
back the unjust and injurious imputations which, without knowledge and
discrimination, he makes against a whole race of people.

This impulse to thrift on the part of the Freedmen was no tardy and reluctant disposition. It was the *immediate* offspring of freedom.

It is not possible even to approximate the landed acquisitions
of the colored people, but that they have been large purchasers of
small holdings will readily be admitted by all candid persons who
are acquainted with the intense pastoral nature of the people,
their constant thrift, and their deepseated determination to own

their own homes. If we assume, with Dr. Crummell, that in the past seventeen years, the hardest, most disadvantageous years they will ever again be compelled to go through, they have come into possession of 5,60,000 acres, the gain in the next seventeen years must be vastly greater. At any rate, we are free to place the holdings in the next fifty years at not less than 35,000,000 acres, and the probability is that it will be vastly more.

In the *Popular Science Monthly* for October 1881, Mr. J. Stahl Patterson, in an article on the "Movement of the Colored Population," says: "It would seem that in the industrial aspects of the case the white and colored men may be, under certain circumstances, the complement of each other." Again: "There are two distinct classes of colored economists. One is satisfied with dependence on others for employment, the other affects independent homes, and struggles to secure them, however humble. Some even acquire wealth."

In the same monthly for February, 1883, Prof. E. W. Gilliam has a long article on the "African in the United States," in which he does all he can to make wider the breach between the blacks and the whites. He has very little good to say of the black man. But he was forced to make the following admissions, viz:

"The blacks are an improving race, and the throb of aspiration is quickening. * * * Advancement in mental training and in economic science must needs be slow but there *is* advancement."

The learned professor makes the interesting calculation that the blacks in the Southern States will increase from 6,000,000 in 1880, to 192,000,000, in 1980; while the whites in the South, in 1880, 12,000,000, will number only 96,000,000, in 1980. The learned professor infers that this vast army will be "doomed to remain where they have been, and be hewers of wood and drawers of water," because they form a "distinct alien race." I think, if the professor will wait until 1980, he will find that this "alien race," which profligate white men have done and are doing so much to amalgamate with their own race, will not only increase

CHAPTER XV

The Land Problem

The ownership of land in the South is the same pernicious thing it has come to be in every civilized country in the world. Instead of being, as it was intended to be, a blessing to the people, it is the crying curse which takes precedence of all other evils that afflict mankind. And the cause is not far to seek. Land is, in its very nature, the common property of the people. Like air and water, it is one of the natural elements which inhere in man as a common right, and without which life could in no wise be sustained. A man must have air, or he will suffocate; he must have water, or he will perish of thirst; he must have access to the soil, for upon it grow those things which nature intended for the sustentation of the physical man, and without which he cannot live. Deprive me of pure fresh air, and I die; deprive me of pure fresh water, and I die; deprive me of free opportunity to earn my bread by the sweat of my brow, by sowing in the sowing time and reaping in the reaping time, and I die. There is no escape from this aspect of the case: there is no logic that can reduce these truisms to sophistries. They are founded in the omnipotent laws of God, and are as universal as the earth. They apply with as much truth to life in the United States as in Dahomey; they operate in like nature upon the savage as upon man in the civilized state. Individual ownership in the land is a transgression of the common right of man, and a usurpation which produces nearly, if not all, the evils which result upon our civilization; the inequalities which produce pauperism, vice, crime, and wide-spread demoralization among all the so-called "lower classes;" which produce, side by side, the millionaire and the tramp, the brownstone front and the hut of the squatter, the wide extending acres of the bonanza farm and the small holding, the lord of the manor and the cringing serf, peasant and slave.

I maintain, with other writers upon this land question, that land is common property, the property of the whole people, and that it cannot be alienated from the people without producing the most fearful consequences. No man is free who is debarred in his right, to so much of the soil of his country as is necessary to support him in his right to life, for without the inherent right to unrestrained access to the soil he cannot support life, except in primitive society where land is plentiful, population sparse, and industry undiversified. As population becomes denser and land becomes scarcer from having been monopolized by the more far seeing, or more fortunate, and industry becomes more diversified, mankind begins to feel the pressure of population described by Malthus, and the scarcity of subsistence; caused, not by this pressure of population, as Malthus maintains, but by the restricted production of subsistence caused by the monopoly and concentration of the soil, which inhibits the producing agency from the production of the increased subsistence necessary to the increased number of mouths to be fed. There can be no such thing as overproduction when there are hundreds and thousands who perish for food; there can be no pressure upon population when there are hundreds and thousands of acres of arable land locked up in a deed purchase, or entail, or primogeniture, upon which alone beasts are allowed to trespass. The idea is preposterous. And yet men who are regarded as standard authority upon economic questions impose this sophistry of overproduction and pressure of population upon mankind, and are applauded for their ignorance, or the cupidity which makes them to pervert the truth.

Monopoly of land is the curse of the race in every modern

government. Being the one great source from which all wealth must and does spring, its concentration in the hands of a few men not only impoverishes the people, but seriously cripples the operations of government (the one and the other being substantially identical) by curtailing the productive energies of the people and diverting into the coffers of individuals rental which should flow into the common treasury as taxes, thus lifting from the shoulders of the people the enormous burden of the maintenance of government which falls upon them.

Monopoly of land was the prime element which hastened the decay of Roman greatness and strength, because when the people no longer had homes to fight for they ceased to be patriots, ceased to be virtuous, and became mercenaries, or slaves or tyrants; left to those who had monopolized the soil, the defense of their property: and these, being few in numbers, parsimonious after the nature of their class, and effeminate from luxurious living and habits of indolence, fell easy victims to the rapacity and iron nerve of Goth and Vandal. The great French Revolution would have never occurred but for the monopoly of land, which, after long ages, became centered in a few hands, who by reason of this were a privileged class and in the refinement of language had been designated as the "nobility." The nobility, as was natural, having been created by the State, not only ground the proletariat to powder but dictated to the State. When it was no longer possible to purchase land, because those whose nobility rested upon it would not alienate it, and when the proletariat had been reduced to a state of vassalage, more vile and grinding than slavery itself, the proletariat rose up in its might and crushed at one tremendous blow the hydra-headed monstrosity. Marat, Danton and Robespierre concentrated in their intense natures the venom, the hate, and the desperation of the people—a more terrible triumvirate than the celebrated one which colored the Tiber with the patrician blood of Rome. The Nihilism of Russia is the outgrowth of monopoly in land and the consequent enslavement of the people by the aristocracy, beginning with the autocrat upon his throne. England has reached a transition period. The pressure of her population has become so intense, that the great producing classes can no longer stand the tension and live. The land has been filched from the people to enrich the brainless favorites and the courtesans of kings, and entailed upon their progeny generation after generation. The land of Great Britain is held by the nobility and the princely cormorants of trade, who exact rental which cannot be paid from the produce of the soil, so usurious is it, or who turn the rich acres into pleasure grounds and pasturages. As Nero fiddled while Rome was one vast blaze of conflagration and horror, so the nobility of Great Britain dance and make merry while the people starve or seek in other lands that opportunity to live which their country denies to them. For the past five years the government of Great Britain has been engaged in a most desperate struggle with the people of one of her constituent islands, the agitation assuming, like the chameleon, different colors or names as the exigencies of the contending forces determined. But the one great question at the root of the agitation is the monopoly of the land by the "nobility" and the successful cormorants of trade, and the consequent pressure of population upon the enforced circumscription of production. The best lands have been alienated from the people, while the inferior lands upon which they are allowed to live will not yield the exorbitant rental demanded and the necessary subsistence for those who work them. Hence, Ireand is in a state so explosive that it can only be appropriately described by the term "dynamitic." In the interest of a few landlords the whole Irish nation has been demoralized and impoverished, so that the government of Great Britain finds it necessary to *"assist"* able-bodied men to reach America, or any other portion of the world they desire to go to, in order to make a living.

If monopoly in land produces such results as these is it not to be condemned as subversive of correct social adjustments and the perpetuity of government? The question admits of but one answer. If monopoly in land compels a government to "assist" its able-bodied men, its laborers, its producers of wealth, its soldiery, to go to other lands, is it not to be condemned as parasitical, destroying the very bone and sinew of government? The answer is self-evident. If monopoly in land produces such results as these, would it not be wise statesmanship and sound governmental policy to confiscate to the people the millions of acres which avarice, cunning, favoritism and robbery have turned into parks, pasturages and game preserves—making the few thousands who constitute the land monopolists, the idlers and the harpies, go honestly to work to make a living, and giving at the same time the same opportunity to the great laboring classes, who earnestly desire to make a living but to whom the opportunity is cruelly and maliciously denied?

I am opposed to aristocracies and so-called privileged classes, because they are opposed to the masses. They make inequalities, out of which grow all the miseries of society, because there is no limit to their avarice, parsimony and cruelty. So *they* thrive, *all the rest* of humanity may go to the dogs; so they revel in luxury and debauchery, all the rest of humanity may revel in poverty, vice and crime; so they enjoy all the blessings of organized society, all the rest of humanity may bear its curses. Man is essentially a selfish animal. Self-preservation is the very first law which he learns to observe and to practice. That he may get on top of the social ladder and remain there, he will sacrifice family, common humanity and patriotism. Naturally, Moloch-self is the god he serves. To enjoy a little brief authority, he would enslave universal mankind, and declare, as Solomon did, after exhausting the catalogue of tyranny and libertinism, "all is vanity"—emptiness! Thus, it is dangerous to confide in the humanity of man. To place in his hands a weapon so all-powerful as land, is to place him upon a pinnacle from whose vast altitude he can, will, and does crush his unfortunate fellowman.

Like the small stream which gathers volume and momentum

in its wanderings from the small lake to the gulf, into which it debouches as a mighty river like the "Father of Waters," so the first encroachments of the land shark are small, and hardly felt; but give him time, let him grow from the Norman soldier of fortune into the English nobility of to-day, and you have a monster whose proportions and rapacity stagger the imagination to fully apprehend. What the common soldier of fortune received as reward for his valor eight hundred years ago, and which he held subject to confiscation to his prince if he failed to render him service in person and with retainers, has developed into a huge monopoly which appropriates in rental more than the tenant can pay, with the added necessary subsistence required to sustain him. There are also the imposition of direct taxes by the government and indirect taxes upon all implements and other articles of manufacture, occasioned by the division of labor, which he must use; all of which taxes the land monopolists have managed to shift upon the tenant and wage-laborer. Time augments the evil. So that, to-day, in Great Britain, a man cannot purchase land, except in rare cases, and then the purchaser must pay a fortune for the privilege. The poor farmer, the wage-laborer, the common man, has not and cannot have any grip upon the soil, but must come into the world a slave, and go down to his grave after a life of toil and self-denial, a slave, with the tormenting consciousness that as he was, so must the unfortunate offspring of his loins be!

If this be the tendency of organized society—if the tendency be to enslave mankind, place a premium upon human woe and crime—then organized society is organized robbery, and the savage state is preferable. There is no appeal from this deduction. What avail the triumphs of art, science and commerce, if the majority of mankind are ground to powder to make those triumphs possible!

It is not the law of God, but the law of man, that produces these herculean evils which constantly threaten the peace and safety of society.

But the British land-owner, having enslaved the people of his own island, has shackled the people of Ireland, Scotland and Wales, doomed them and their posterity to be perpetual aliens in their native lands; he has, upon the plea of conquest, the argument of the base assassin and robber, reduced the people of India to a state worse than death; and his iron grip has been placed upon the uncounted millions of African soil; the Islands of the sea squirm in his grasp; the West India Islands are his prostrate prey; while a portion of the vast continent of America owns his sway and groans under his exactions.

But this is not all. In our own country the British land shark has made his appearance. His vile clutch, which our forefathers unwrenched in the strength of their Colonial greatness, has again been fastened upon our throat. The following table will show the extent to which the parasite has insinuated himself into our vital parts. Let the good people of this country—who should know that monopoly in land is the death note of free institutions; that large estates are the parasites of republics and the death of small freeholders—let the people read the following table with the closeness which its gravity should inspire. The San Francisco *Daily Examiner*, a leading paper on the Pacific coast says:

Besides the millions of acres belonging to railroad and other corporations, the amount of land that is being acquired by foreign capitalists and landlords is fairly amazing. Ireland is to-day groaning beneath the yoke of oppression, and not many years will roll around before the American tenant, upon his knees, will also look up into the scowling face of his master and acknowledge his obedience. Following are a few of America's foreign landlords, and the amount of their holdings expressed in acres:—

An English Syndicate, No. 3, in Texas	3,000,000
The Holland Land Company, New Mexico	4,500,000
Sir Edward Reid, and a syndicate in Florida	2,000,000
English Syndicate, in Mississippi	1,800,000
Marquis of Tweedale	1,750,000
Philips, Marshal & Co., London	1,300,000
German Syndicate	1,100,000
Anglo-American Syndicate, Mr. Rogers President, London	750,000
Byron H. Evans, of London, in Mississippi	700,000
Duke of Sutherland	425,000

British Land Company, in Kansas	320,000
William Whallay, M. P., Peterboro, England	310,000
Missouri Land Company, Edinburgh, Scotland	300,000
Robert Tennant, of London	230,000
Dundee Land Company, Scotland	247,000
Lord Dunmore	120,000
Benjamin Newgas, Liverpool	100,000
Lord Houghton, in Florida	60,000
Lord Dunraven, in Colorado	60,000
English Land Company, in Florida	50,000
English Land Company, in Arkansas	50,000
Albert Peel, M. P., Leicestershire, England	10,000
Sir J. L. Kay, Yorkshire, England	5,000
Alexander Grant, of London, in Kansas	35,000
English Syndicate (represented by Closs Bros.) Wisconsin	110,000
M. Ellerhauser, of Halifax, Nova Scotia, in West Virginia	600,000
A Scotch Syndicate, in Florida	500,000
A. Boysen, Danish Consul, in Milwaukee	50,000
Missouri Land Company, of Edinburgh, Scotland	165,000
Total	20,747,000

Commenting upon these startling figures, the *New York (Daily) World,* one of the best informed papers of the time says:

The land grabber is not a fungus of nineteenth century growth. He first came among English-speaking peoples over eight centuries ago. Wherever his foot has found a standing-place pauperism and its sequence, crime, have followed. In the British Isles he is known as an Acreocrat. Since he has extended his operations from his native country to our own free soil the land-grabber should be examined under the microscope of history analytically, impartially, and truthfully.

The unnaturalized foreigner threatens us with other dangers than those which would be created by our indigenous American land-grabber. The British acreocrat who owns real estate in this country believes in the cancer of English monarchy with its hideous annals of nearly a thousand years. He accepts the tradition of an hereditary House of Lords, a body composed of the effete and played out descendants of the most tyrannical and profligate rascals which Europe ever produced, and he will remain an English blueblood in every thought and action, which cannot fail to bring about in free America and on his own acres here the same poverty-stricken class of peasants as now curse Great Britain and Ireland.

English "upper-tendom" is represented in recent purchases of American soil by one duke, one marquis, two earls, a baron, two baronets and two members of Parliament. The British duke owns 425,000 acres; the marquis, 1,750,-000 acres; the two earls, 160,000 acres; the baron, 60,000 acres; the brace of baronets, 2,000,500 acres; and the pair of Parliamentary politicians, 860,000 acres. In the rest of the land purchased by our brand-new imported lords of the soil, England's governing acreocrats, are largely represented in their 20,941,666 acres.

Much ignorance is affected in American society respecting the manner in which the British landocrats came by their property. It is enough that "my lud" has a handle to his name, and Murray Hill shoddyocracy will wine and dine and toady him, and perhaps for his title marry him to some sweet, pure and good American girl, whose life hereafter will be a purgatory to herself and a mutual misery to both.

But the land held by the foreigner in the United States is a mere bagatelle. He is odious not because he is a foreigner, but only because he is the representative, on the one hand, of the odious land system of the Old World, and on the other of those monarchical ideas which have made the great body of the European people unwilling slaves, reducing them to the very verge of desperation and starvation. Archimedes explained, as illustrating the vast power of the fulcrum, that if he had a place to stand he could move the world. The British land-shark, having got his hold upon the soil, possesses the place to stand for which the Greek sighed in vain, and no man will say he does not move the world; and he will continue to move *it* until such time as the world shall move *him*.

The foreign land-shark is still in his infancy. We have an indigenous land-shark whose maw is so capacious that the rapacity of his appetite in no wise keeps pace with its lightning-like digestion. Congressman William Steel Holman, of Indiana, one of the purest statesmen of these corrupt times, and one of the most thoroughly informed men of the country upon the question of eminent domain, and the bestowal of that domain upon corporations and syndicates, recently said, on the floor of the House of Representatives, in the course of a discussion on the Post-office Appropriation bill:

Is it just and proper to require the landgrant railroads to transport your mails at 50 per cent of the rates you pay to corporations whose railroads were built by private capital? I think it is. I think it liberal and more than liberal when the cost in public wealth is considered in the building of these land-grant railroads. I submit tables of the railroads built under the land-grant system, compiled from official reports, and they show an aggregate of 218,-386,199 acres, 192,081,155 acres of which were granted between June 30, 1862, and March 4, 1875, the aggregate length of railroads for which the grants were made being 20,803 miles, 13,071 miles independent of the 7,732 mileage of the Pacific roads; and the reports of the Post-office Department show that last year the Government paid, on 11,588,56 miles of land-grant railroad, independent of the Union Pacific system and the great body of lapsed grants, $1,144,323.91 for postal service. The startling fact appears that in the gradual development of these grants, great as they are, they still swell in their proportions. I pointed out on a former occasion the startling discrepancies that appear in the official statements of these grants, and can only say now, as I did then, that in such enormous grants a few million acres either way is considered of no moment.

Again:

There are other grants which I have not included in either of the foregoing tables where not a spadeful of earth has been dug in the construction of a railroad, yet the lands are withdrawn from settlement and claimed by the corporation, although the grants were long since forfeited. The forfeiture of these grants will, of course, be declared. Of all of these grants over 109,000,-000 acres, including over 16,000,000 this House has already declared forfeited, are beyond any reasonable question forfeited, and the declaration of that forfeiture by Congress is demanded by the highest consideration of public policy, common honesty, and justice to the people. Even to the extent these land-grant railroads enumerated in the first table were completed, you paid them, as I have shown, last year $1,144,323.91 for transporting your mails. This bill would, as to these roads, to the extent they are entitled to the lands granted and including the Pacific systems, save to the Treasury annually, I think, near a million dollars, perhaps more.

Deducing from the foregoing statement of land-grants to corporations, Mr. Holman draws the following picture of what the people may do when they are fully informed and aroused to the enormous extent to which they have been despoiled by their unfaithful servants in congress:

The wealth that builds palaces, undermines the foundations of free Government, and wrings from the heart of labor the cry of despair! With the public lands exhausted, with remnants of the Indian-tribes despoiled of their reservations, and the lands seized upon by capitalists and merciless speculators (except so far as you have pledged them in advance to the railroad corporations), and lands everywhere advanced in price beyond the reach of laboring men, with the hope of better fortune and of independent homes dying out of the heart of labor, with men fully conscious of the wrong you have done them by your legislation, can the peaceful order of society be hoped for as of old? I am not astonished that gentlemen deem this early hour an opportune moment to urge the policy of a great navy; it will come, if it does come, in the natural order before a great army. Capital is timid and full of suggestions; the Navy is the most remote, but I am not surprised that here and there comes also the intimation that your Army is too small. These, too, may be some of the bitter fruits of your imperial grants. I fear that it will be seen soon enough that when you have destroyed the very foundations of security and hope upon which labor has rested so long, the old-time repose and peaceful order will be no more. Gentlemen should not forget that the wrong that has been done to laboring men and their children by giving over their natural inheritance to an accursed monopoly will in due time be considered by the most intelligent body of laboring men who ever debated a public wrong—men fully aware of their rights and capable of asserting them.

But the foreign land-shark, and the corporate land-shark, dwindle into insignificance by the side of the individual land-shark. Every hamlet, town, city, and state in the Union is in the grasp of the individual land holder. Starting with his fellows as a pioneer two hundred and fifty years ago, with his pickaxe on his shoulder, he has steadily grown in size and importance, so that today he holds in his hands the destinies of the Republic and the life of his fellow citizens. His bulk has become mastodonian in proportions and his influence has shrivelled up the energies of the people. More absolute than the Iron Prince of Germany, he pays no taxes; he limits production, not to the requirements of the population but to the demand of the market, at such figures as he can extort from the crying necessities of the people through the operations of "corners;" he regulates the wheels of government, State and Federal, and dictates to the people by making them hungry and naked.

We stand only upon the threshold of governmental existence; the nation, in comparison to the hoary-handed commonwealths of

Europe, was born but yesterday; but, having adopted at the beginning the system which hastened the downfall of Rome after
she had spread her authority over the known world, we are already weak and exhausted. Monopoly has stunted the people, and
they stagger to the grave, starved to death by a system of robbery
almost too transparent to require minute elucidation at the hand
of the conscientious writer upon economic questions. The sup-
pressed groans of the toiling masses are echoed and reëchoed
from every corner of the land, and burst forth in mobocratic fury
that the entire police authority finds it almost impossible to stay.
The newspapers are a daily chronicle of the desperate condition
to which the country has been brought by the rapacity and ignorance of legislators and the parasitical manipulations of the gang
which has rooted itself in the soil of the country.

The fires of revolution are incorporated into the *Magna Charta*
of our liberties, and no human power can avert the awful eruption
which will eventually burst upon us as Mount Vesuvius burst forth
upon Herculaneum and Pompeii. It is too late for America to be
wise in time. *"The die is cast."*

CHAPTER XVI

Conclusion

I know it is not fashionable for writers on economic questions to tell the truth, but the truth should be told, though it kill. When the wail of distress encircles the world, the man who is linked by "the touch of nature" which "makes the whole world kin" to the common destiny of the race universal; who hates injustice wherever it lifts up its head; who sympathizes with the distressed, the weak, and the friendless in every corner of the globe, such a man is morally bound to tell the truth as he conceives it to be the truth.

In these times, when the law-making and enforcing authority is leagued against the people; when great periodicals—monthly, weekly and daily—echo the mandates or anticipate the wishes of the powerful men who produce our social demoralization, it becomes necessary for the few men who do not agree to the arguments advanced or the interests sought to be bolstered up, to "cry aloud and spare not." The man who with the truth in his possession flatters with lies, that "thrift may follow fawning" is too vile to merit the contempt of honest men.

The government of the United States confiscated as "contraband of war" the slave population of the South, but it left to the portion of the unrepentant rebel a far more valuable species of property. The slave, the perishable wealth, was confiscated to the government and then manumitted; but property in land, the wealth which perishes not nor can fly away, and which had made the institution of slavery possible, was left as the heritage of the robber who had not hesitated to lift his iconoclastic hand against the liberties of his country. The baron of feudal Europe would have been paralyzed with astonishment at the leniency of the conquering invader who should take from him his slave, subject to mutation, and leave him his landed possessions which are as fixed as the Universe of Nature. He would ask no more advantageous concession. But the United States took the slave and left the thing which gave birth to *chattel slavery* and which is now fast giving birth to *industrial slavery*; a slavery more excruciating in its exactions, more irresponsible in its machinations than that other slavery, which I once endured. The chattel slave-holder must, to preserve the value of his property, feed, clothe and house his property, and give it proper medical attention when disease or accident threatened its life. But industrial slavery requires no such care. The new slave-holder is only solicitous of obtaining the maximum of labor for the minimum of cost. He does not regard the man as of any consequence when he can no longer produce. Having worked him to death, or ruined his constitution and robbed him of his labor, he turns him out upon the world to live upon the charity of mankind or to die of inattention and starvation. He knows that it profits him nothing to waste time and money upon a disabled industrial slave. The multitude of laborers from which he can recruit his necessary laboring force is so enormous that solicitude on his part for one that falls by the wayside would be a gratuitous expenditure of humanity and charity which the world is too intensely selfish and materialistic to expect him. Here he forges wealth and death at one and the same time. He could not do this if our social system did not confer upon him a monopoly of the soil from which subsistence must be derived, because the industrial slave, given an equal opportunity to produce for himself, would not produce for another. On the other hand the large industrial operations, with the multitude of laborers from which Adam Smith declares employers grow rich, as far as this applies to the soil, would not be possible, since the vast volume of increased production brought about by the industry of the multitude of co-equal small farmers would so reduce the cost price of food products as to destroy the incentive to speculation in them, and at the same time utterly destroy the necessity or the possibility of famines, such as those which have from time to time come upon the Irish people. There could be no famine, in the natural course of things, where all had an opportunity to cultivate as much land as they could wherever they found any not already under cultivation by some one else. It needs no stretch of the imagination to see what a startling tendency the announcement that all vacant land was free to settlement upon condition of cultivation would have to the depopulation of over-crowded cities like New York, Baltimore and Savannah, where the so-called pressure of population upon subsistence has produced a hand-to-hand fight for existence by the wage-workers in every avenue of industry.

This is no fancy picture. It is a plain, logical deduction of what would result from the restoration to the people of that equal chance in the race of life which every man has a right to expect, to demand, and to exact as a condition of his membership of organized society.

The wag who started the "forty acres and a mule" idea among the black people of the South was a wise fool; wise in that he enunciated a principle which every argument of sound policy should have dictated, *upon the condition that the forty acres could in no wise be alienated,* and that it could be regarded *only* as *property* as *long as it was cultivated;* and a fool because he designed simply to impose upon the credulity and ignorance of his victims. But the justness of the "forty acre" donation cannot be controverted. In the first place, the slave had earned this miserable stipend from the government by two hundred years of unrequited toil; and, secondly, as a free man, he was inherently entitled to so much of the soil of his country as would suffice to maintain him in the freedom thrust upon him. To tell him he was a free man, and at the same time shut him off from free access to the soil upon which he had been reared, without a penny in his pocket, and with an army of children at his coat-tail—some of his reputed wife's children being the illegitimate offspring of a former inhuman master—was to add insult to injury, to mix syrup and hyssop, to aggravate into curses the pretended conferrence of blessings.

When I think of the absolutely destitute condition of the colored people of the South at the close of the Rebellion; when I remember the moral and intellectual enervation which slavery had produced in them; when I remember that not only were they thus bankrupt, but that they were absolutely and unconditionally cut off from the soil, with absolutely no right or title in it, I am surprised,—not that they have already got a respectable slice of landed interests; not that they have taken hold eagerly of the advantages of moral and intellectual opportunities of development placed in their reach by the charitable philanthropy of good men and women; not that they have bought homes and supplied them with articles of convenience and comfort, often of luxury—but I am surprised that the race did not turn robbers and highwaymen, and, in turn, terrorize and rob society as society had for so long terrorized and robbed them. The thing is strange, marvelous, phenomenal in the extreme. Instead of becoming outlaws, as the critical condition would seem to have indicated, the black men of the South *went manfully to work* to better their own condition and the crippled condition of the country which had been produced by the ravages of internecine rebellion; *while the white men of the South, the capitalists, the land-sharks, the poor white trash, and the nondescripts, with a thousand years of Christian civilization and culture behind them, with "the boast of chivalry, the pomp of power," these white scamps, who had imposed upon the world the idea that they were paragons of virtue and the heaven-sent vicegerents of civil power, organized themselves into a band of outlaws, whose concatenative chain of auxiliaries ran through the entire South, and deliberately proceeded to murder innocent men and women for* POLITICAL REASONS *and to systematically rob them of their honest labor because they were too accursedly lazy to labor themselves.*

But this highly abnormal, unnatural condition of things is fast passing away. The white man having asserted his superiority in the matters of assassination and robbery, has settled down upon a barrel of dynamite, as he did in the days of slavery, and will await the explosion with the same fatuity and self-satisfaction true of him in other days. But as convulsions from within are more violent and destructive than convulsions from without, being more deepseated and therefore more difficult to reach, the next explosion will be more disastrous, more far-reaching in its havoc than the one which metamorphosed social conditions in the South, and from the dreadful reactions of which we are just now recovering.

As I have said elsewhere, the future struggle in the South will be, not between white men and black men, but between capital and labor, landlord and tenant. Already the cohorts are marshalling to the fray; already the forces are mustering to the field at the sound of the slogan.

The same battle will be fought upon Southern soil that is in preparation in other states where the conditions are older in development but no more deep-seated, no more pernicious, no more blighting upon the industries of the country and the growth of the people.

It is not my purpose here to enter into an extended analysis of the foundations upon which our land system rests, nor to give my views as to how matters might be remedied. I may take up the question at some future time. It is sufficient for my purpose to have indicated that the social problems in the South, as they exfoliate more and more as resultant upon the war, will be found to be the same as those found in every other section of our country; and to have pointed out that the questions of "race," "condition" "politics," etc., will all properly adjust themselves with the advancement of the people in wealth, education, and forgetfulness of the unhappy past.

The hour is approaching when the laboring classes of our country, North, East, West and South, will recognize that they have a *common cause*, a *common humanity* and a *common enemy*; and that, therefore, if they would triumph over wrong and place the laurel wreath upon triumphant justice, without distinction of race or of previous condition *they must unite!* And unite they will, for "a fellow feeling makes us wond'rous kind." When the issue is properly joined, the rich, be they black or be they white, will be found upon the same side; and the poor, be they black or be they white, will be found on the same side.

Necessity knows no law and discriminates in favor of no man or race.

APPENDIX

I append to this volume a portion of the testimony of Mr. John Caldwell Calhoun because of the uniform fairness with which he treated the race and labor problem in the section of country where he is an extensive landowner and employer of labor.

Mr. Calhoun's testimony was given before the Blair Senate Committee on Education and Labor and will be found in the Committee's Report as to *The Relations between Labor and Capital.* (Vol. II, pp. 157).

NEW YORK, *Thursday, September* 13, 1883

LABOR IN THE SOUTHWEST

JOHN CALDWELL CALHOUN sworn and examined

By the CHAIRMAN:

Question. Where do you reside?—Answer. In Chicot County, Arkansas.

Q. State to the committee, if you please, where you were born, of what family connection you are, and what have been your opportunities for becoming acquainted with the past and the present condition of agricultural labor in the Southern States.—A. I was born in Marengo County, Alabama. My father was a planter there before the war.

Q. He was a son of John C. Calhoun, the statesman?—A. He was a son of Mr. John C. Calhoun, of South Carolina.

Q. You are his grandson, then?—A. Yes, sir; I am his grandson. My father was Col. Andrew P. Calhoun. I was reared in South Carolina. In 1854 my father removed his residence from his plantations in Alabama to

Fort Hill, South Carolina, near Pendleton, where I was raised. I have been identified with the agricultural interest of the South from my earliest recollections, and have been a practical cotton planter myself since the war, giving my own personal attention to my interests since 1869.

Q. When did you remove from South Carolina?—A. I removed from South Carolina to Chicot County, Arkansas, in 1869.

Q. Until 1869 you had been a resident of South Carolina?—A. Yes, sir.

Q. And of course very familiar with the condition of things on the Atlantic coast. Since that time you have been in the Mississippi Valley?— A. Yes, sir; my experience as a cotton planter and with the laborers of the South is confirmed, I may say, almost entirely to the Mississippi Valley, for I left South Carolina so soon after the war that things had hardly shaped themselves there so that I could form an accurate estimate of the labor or the condition of affairs in South Carolina or on the Atlantic coast.

The CHAIRMAN. Not having had a personal acquaintance with Mr. Calhoun, and learning of his rare opportunities to give valuable information to the committee, and of his presence in the city, I addressed him a letter, calling attention to the subject-matter upon which we should like information, and which I had reason to think he could give us better than almost any one else, indicating certain questions which I would like to have him prepared to answer, and receiving a courteous reply, expressing a willingness to oblige the committee, I have called him before the committee, and will now read the questions:—

1st. What is the condition of the laborers in your section?

2d. Under what system are the laborers in your section employed?

3d. When hired for wages what is paid?

4th. What division is made between labor and capital of their joint production when you work on shares?

5th. When you rent what division is made?

6th. How many hours do the laborers work?

7th. Under what system do you work?

8th. What is the relation existing between the planters and their employees?

9th. What danger is there of strikes?

10th. How can the interest of the laborers of your section be best subserved?

If you have prepared answers to these questions, and can give your answers consecutively, I would like you to do so.

The WITNESS. I have prepared replies in order that I might save the committee time as well as condense my ideas.

Q. 1. What is the condition of the laborers in your section?—A. The laborers in the Mississippi Valley are agricultural. But few whites are employed; they soon become landowners or tenants. Your question, therefore, reduces itself to, What is the condition of the negroes? I should say good, as compared with a few years ago, and improving. You must recollect that it has only been 18 years since the negroes emerged from slavery without a dollar and with no education, and that for generations they had been taught to rely entirely upon others for guidance and support. They became, therefore, at once the easy prey of unscrupulous men, who used them for their personal aggrandizement, were subjected to every evil influence, and did not discover for years the impositions practiced upon them. They were indolent and extravagant, and eager to buy on a credit everything the planter or merchant would sell them. The planter had nothing except the land, which, with the crop to be grown, was mortgaged generally for advances. If he refused to indulge his laborers in extravagant habits during the year, by crediting them for articles not absolutely necessary, his action was regarded as good grounds for them to quit work, and there were those present who were always ready to use this as an argument to array the negroes against the proprietors. This, of course, demoralized the country to a very great extent, and it has only been in the past few years the negro laborers have realized their true condition and gone to work with a view of making a support for themselves and families. There is yet much room for improvement, but they will improve just as they gain experience and become self-reliant.

Considering their condition after emancipation and the evil influences to which they have been subjected, even the small advancement they have made seems surprising.

Q. 2. Under what systems are the laborers in your section employed?— A. There are three methods: we hire for wages, for a part of the crop, or we rent.

Q. 3. When hired for wages what is paid?—A. When hired by the month we pay unskilled field hands from $10 to $20 per month and board. When hired by the day, for unskilled laborers, from 75 cents to $1. Teamsters, $1 a day and board. Artisans, from $2 to $5. In addition to their wages and board, the laborers are furnished, free of cost, a house, fuel, and a garden spot varying from half to one acre; also the use of wagon and team with which to haul their fuel and supplies, and pasturage, where they have cattle and hogs, which they are encouraged to raise.

Q. 4. What division is made between labor and capital of their joint production when you work on shares?—A. I doubt if there is greater liberality shown to laborers in any portion of the world than is done under this system. The proprietor furnishes the land and houses, including dwelling, stables, and outhouses, pays the taxes, makes all necessary improvements, keeps up repairs and insurance, gives free of cost a garden spot, fuel, pasturage for the stock owned by the laborer, and allows the use of his teams for hauling fuel and family supplies, provides mules or horses, wagons, gears, implements, feed for teams, the necessary machinery for ginning, or, in short, every expense of making the crop and preparing it for market, and then divides equally the whole gross proceeds with the laborers. In addition to all this, the proprietor frequently mortgages his real estate to obtain means to advance to the laborers supplies on their portion of the crop yet to be grown, thus mortgaging what he actually possesses, and taking a security not yet in existence, and which depends not only upon the vicissitudes of the seasons, but the faithfulness of the laborers themselves. Under this system thrifty, industrious laborers ought soon to become landowners. But, owing to indolence, the negroes, except where they are very judiciously managed and encouraged, fail to take advantage of the opportunities offered them to raise the necessaries of life. They idle away all the time not actually necessary to make and gather their corn and cotton, and improvidently spend what balance may remain after paying for the advances made to them.

Q. 5. When you rent, what division is made?—A. Where the laborer owns his own teams, gears, and implements necessary for making a crop, he gets two-thirds or three-fourths of the crop, according to the quality and location of the land.

Under the rental system proper, where a laborer is responsible and owns his team, &c., first-class land is rented to him for $8 or $10 per acre. With the land go certain privileges, such as those heretofore enumerated.

Q. 6. How many hours do the laborers work?—A. This is an extremely difficult question to answer. Under the wages system, from sunrise to sunset, with a rest for dinner of from one and one-half to three hours, according to the season of the year.

Under the share or rental system there is much time lost; for instance, they seldom work on Saturday at all, and as the land is fertile, and a living can be made on a much smaller acreage than a hand can cultivate, they generally choose one-third less than they should, and it is safe to say that one third of the time which could and would be utilized by an industrious laborer is wasted in fishing, and hunting, and idleness.

Q. 7. Under what system do you work?—A. We are forced to adopt all systems heretofore stated. We prefer, however, the tenant system. We wish to make small farmers our laborers, and bring them up as nearly as possible to the standard of the small white farmers. But this can only be done gradually, because the larger portion of the negroes are without any personal property. We could not afford to sell the mules, implements, &c., where a laborer has nothing. Therefore the first year we contract to work with him on the half-share system, and require him to plant a portion of the land he cultivates in corn, hay, potatoes, &c. For this portion we charge him a reasonable rent, to be paid out of his part of the cotton raised on the remainder. In this way all of the supplies raised belong to him, and at the end of the first year he will, if industrious, find himself possessed of enough supplies to support and feed a mule. We then sell him a mule and implements, preserving, of course, liens until paid. At the end of the second year, if he should be unfortunate, and not quite pay out, we carry the balance over to the next year, and in this way we gradually make a tenant of him. We encourage him in every way in our power to be economical, industrious, and prudent, to surround his home with comforts, to plant an orchard and garden, and to raise his own meat, and to keep his own cows, for which he has free pasturage. Our object is to attach him as much as possible to his home. Under whatever system we work, we require the laborer to plant a part of his land in food crops and the balance in cotton with which to pay his rent and give him ready money. We consider this system as best calculated to advance him. Recognizing him as a citizen, we think we should do all in our power to fit him for the duties of citizenship. We think there is no better method of doing this than by interesting him in the production of the soil, surrounding him with home comforts, and imposing upon him the responsibilities of his business. Who will make the best citizen or laborer, he who goes to a home with a week's rations, wages spent, wife and children hired out, or he who returns to a home surrounded with the ordinary comforts, and wife and children helping him to enjoy the products of their joint labor? We recognize that no country can be prosperous unless the farmers are prosperous. Under our system, we seek to have our property cultivated by a reliable set of tenants, who will be able to always pay their rent and have a surplus left.

Again, a large portion of the cotton crop of the country is made by small white farmers. These to a great extent are raising their own supplies, and making cotton a surplus crop. The number who do this will increase year by year. It must be apparent that the large planters cannot afford to hire labor and compete with those whose cotton costs nothing except the expenditure of their own muscle and energy. The natural consequence resulting from this condition of things is that the negro, if he is to prosper, must gradually become a small farmer, either as a tenant or the owner of the soil, and look himself upon cotton as a surplus crop.

Q. 8. What is the relation existing between the planters and their employers?—A. Friendly and harmonious. The planter feel an interest in the welfare of his laborers, and the latter in turn look to him for advice and assistance.

Q. 9. What danger is there of strikes?—A. Very little. As a rule the laborers are interested in the production of the soil, and a strike would be as disastrous to them as it would be to the proprietors. There is really very little conflict between labor and capital. The conflict in my section, if any should come in future, will not assume the form of labor against capital, but of race against race.

Q. 10. How can the interest of the laborers of your section be best subserved?—A. By the establishment by the States of industrial schools, by the total elimination from Federal politics of the so-called negro question, and by leaving the solution to time, and a reduction of taxation, both indirect and incidental. It is a noteworthy fact that the improvement of my section has kept pace, *pari passu,* with the cessation of the agitation of race issues. The laborers share equally with the landowners the advantages of the improvement, and there is every reason to expect increasing and permanent prosperity if all questions between the landowners and their laborers in our section are left to the natural adjustment of the demand for labor. For many years the negroes regarded themselves as the wards of the Federal Government, and it were well for them to understand that they have nothing more to expect from the Federal Government, than the white man, and that, like him, their future depends upon their own energy, industry, and economy. This can work no hardship. The constant demand for labor affords them the amplest protection. Nothing, probably, would contribute so immediately to their prosperity as the reduction of the tariff. They are the producers of no protected articles. The onerous burdens of the tariff naturally fall heaviest upon those who are large consumers of protected articles and produce only the great staples, grain and cotton, which form the basis of our export trade, and which can, from their very nature in this country, receive no protection from a tariff.

Q. In your own State, Arkansas, what portion of the land cultivated and what proportion of the acreage of the land cultivated is in the form of large plantations?—A. That lying along the Mississippi and Arkansas Rivers. It would be hard for me to estimate the proportions. I do not know that I have ever considered it, but the portions which are cultivated in large plantations lie directly on the Mississippi River in front of the State of Arkansas and on the Arkansas River. The rest of the State is cultivated very much by small white farmers.

Q. And are the productions of the small holdings and large holdings similar; I inquire as to cotton particularly?—A. No, sir. In the interior of the State cotton is made a surplus crop entirely.

Q. What are the principal crops there?—A. Our people are raising their own supplies, fruits and vegetables. For instance, it was stated by the land agent of the Iron Mountain Railroad at a public meeting in Little Rock some weeks ago that that road had carried out from the State of Arkansas in one week 800,000 pounds of green peas and strawberries.

Q. To what market?—A. To Saint Louis, going to different markets. The section of the State lying between Little Rock and Fort Smith is peculiarly adapted for growing fruit, and there is a very large fruit trade.

Q. What kinds of fruit?—A. I might say almost all kinds, but particularly apples; that section of country is noted for its apples.

Q. Are peaches raised there also?—A. Very fine, indeed.

Q. Plums?—A. Yes, sir.

Q. Are oranges raised there?—A. No, sir; we do not raise any of the tropical fruits, such as oranges, bananas, and lemons.

Q. How in regard to oats, rye, corn, wheat, potatoes, and crops of that description?—A. If our exhibit, which is now being made at the Louisville Exposition, can be seen it will compare favorably with that of any other portion of the United States.

Q. Even with the Northwest?—A. Even with the Northwest.

Q. Would you judge that one-half the cultivated surface of Arkansas is made up of the larger plantations?—A. No, sir; I should not say more than a third, as a rough estimate.

Q. Upon these plantations is there any crop raised for consumption anywhere but upon the plantations, save the cotton?—A. Only in a very limited way. We raise Irish potatoes for the northern markets, and it is an extremely profitable and productive crop with us.

Q. What is the home market price?—A. We do not sell these potatoes at home at all. We get them to Saint Louis, Chicago, and Cincinnati before the ground is really thawed out up there. We get from $5 to $10 a barrel for them.

Q. A barrel of about 3 bushels?—A. A barrel of about 3 bushels. That of course is a fancy price, and only lasts until the product comes in from other sources.

Q. That is an advantage no farmer has elsewhere in the United States than in Arkansas?—A. In Arkansas and Louisiana, on the Mississippi River.

Q. Are potatoes raised largely in Louisiana?—A. Yes, sir; in parts. The cultivation of the alluvial lands in Louisiana is very similar to what I am speaking of in Arkansas.

Q. Is the potato of good quality raised on those rich lands?—A. Of very fine quality.

Q. Can you give the average crop of potatoes per acre?—A. I cannot, as I have never raised any myself for market. We leave it almost entirely to our small farmers to do that sort of thing.

Q. About 300 bushels per acre, Senator Pugh says. This is the Irish potato you speak of, not the sweet?—A. The Irish potato. We raise also the sweet potato there. I have raised sweet potatoes that weighed five pounds.

Q. And of good quality?—A. Of fine quality.

Q. The size does not depreciate the quality, then?—A. Not at all.

Q. They, I suppose are raised for exportation from the State?—A. No, sir; they are raised almost entirely for home consumption by our farmers.

Q. Do your people at home prefer the sweet to the Irish potato for their own use?—A. I cannot say they do. I think they raise both in equal proportions.

Q. Which, on the whole, is the most profitable crop to raise of potatoes? —A. The Irish potatoes because we export and sell them. The sweet potato does not mature until the fall of the year.

Q. Upon your plantations you encourage the raising of the variety of crops you have spoken of for consumption, by the laborers, and for the use of the planter, I suppose, but not for exportation and sale?—A. Not for sale. We merely raise them for home consumption in case of a disaster to our cotton crops. The cotton crop is subjected to very many vicissitudes, and we want to have all our supplies at home, so that in case of a failure of the cotton crop we have our living made at least.

Q. Are the planters and those who labor upon the plantations substantially independent of the small farmers surrounding them, or do they constitute consumers for the smaller farmers in the interior?—A. We have our own gardens, and generally raise our own supplies, but every planter interests himself to find a market for all the products of his laborers. For instance, we encourage them to raise poultry to a great extent. If they have a surplus of potatoes, or eggs, or chickens, we will buy it and create a market for it, and ship the articles off in order that if they have any surplus they may realize on it. On the Mississippi River we have nearly all the markets. Boats are passing there every day going directly by the banks of the river. We have the markets of New Orleans, Vicksburg, Memphis, Saint Louis, Chicago, and we have, you may say, the whole country open before us where we can create a market. We make the best market we can for the products of our small farmers.

Q. Do you know something of the prices in the North for the various crops you have mentioned, and if so, how do they compare with the price realized by your laborers at home?—A. Our laborers realize the prices of the Northwest. We ship the articles for them. For instance, a negro has several barrels of potatoes; I consign them to my merchants in Saint Louis, and have them sold for his account.

Q. There are no middlemen, really; you transact this business for them?—A. I transact this business for them direct.

Q. Charging them simply the cost of transportation?—A. You are asking me the relationship between the proprietor and the negro. There are a great many stores on the Mississippi River, and negroes sometimes go and trade directly. There are a great many properties in the Mississippi Valley owned by non-residents. There are some plantations rented out to negroes that there is not a white man on at all. The proprietor comes and collects his rent at the end of the year when the crop is made; or it may be his negro tenant consigns the cotton to a factor in New Orleans.

Q. Where is the proprietor himself usually resident?—A. In different States. We have people who are proprietors of real estate who live out in Orange, New Jersey; some live in South Carolina; some live in Georgia, in the various States, but they own property with us, and this property is rented directly to the negroes. Generally, though, there is a responsible manager in charge of this property, but there are instances where there is not even a white man on the place at all.

Q. In those instances, how do matters work? Do the negroes conduct affairs with reasonable prudence, and consult the interest of the owners? —A. No, sir; in these instances the property generally goes to decay gradually; the negro will not make an improvement on real estate at all.

Q. In these cases do the negroes work together and carry on the plantation as a whole, or is the plantation cut up into small holdings and rented out to negroes?—A. It is cut into small portions and rented according to the size of the family. Some men work two mules; some four. It is regulated better by the number of animals he works. For instance, a mule can cultivate in that country with ease about fifteen acres. A man with two mules would work thirty acres; a man with four, sixty, and so on. I know some negroes who work eight and ten mules that they have paid for; but I will say this right here, and it shows the necessity of the education of the negro and of fitting him for the condition of being able to take care of himself and make his own contracts and sign his own name to a contract: I have known of numerous instances where negroes, working under the management of a proprietor of a plantation, have made enough money to buy a home; such a one will go back out in the hills, that section of country lying back of the alluvial lands, and buy a home. In three or four years he will move back to the river again, having lost all his property, mortgaged it to some storekeeper, become extravagant, and that storekeeper in a short time—three or four years probably—will have absorbed all he had earned under the management of a planter.

Q. About that store system; how extensive is it, and how great an evil does it constitute?—A. It constitutes a very considerable evil, but you cannot blame the storekeeper for it, for this reason, or he can only be blamed partially: Capital in that country is very limited. When you consider the fact that New Orleans, which handles the cotton crop of that country, has a smaller banking capital than any one of your little towns in Massachusetts or New Hampshire, it shows at once that there is not enough capital to be advanced to the country people at reasonable enough rates of interest for those people to conduct a strictly legitimate business. I have known capital to cost in New Orleans, counting the commissions, 15 or 20 per cent, for money loaned. The storekeeper who borrows money to conduct his business with has to buy his goods from some merchant at some point who must make his profit. He cannot go directly to the producer, because he has got to have somebody to help him out if his capital falls short. Therefore, before the goods get down to him, they cost him perhaps 30, 40, or 50 percent more than the first price. Therefore he has to tack on an enormous profit to bring himself out whole and pay his expenses in order to meet his obligations with the factor in New Orleans. There is, however, among a certain class, as there would be in all sections of the country, as exists right here in New York, or anywhere else, a set of people who will always prey upon ignorance. The best protection that can be afforded to the laborer of that country is education; fit him for his condition of life, that he may protect himself.

Q. Do you mean to be understood that these traders do business upon borrowed capital?—A. Almost entirely.

Q. Their capital is hired in New Orleans?—A. Or any points they may go for it; I merely mention New Orleans as one point. A number of our people borrow money in Memphis, and some borrow money in Vicksburg.

Q. Do you know whether those people to any extent borrow capital of Northern capitalists in New York and other portions of the North—A. That class of people do not. In the last few years—I might say almost within the last two years—Northern capital has begun to seek investment in our section of the country, but only upon mortgages on real estate. The class of storekeepers I allude to generally have no real estate at all; they only have their stores.

Q. Your system by which the planter makes a market for the surplus productions of the laborers upon his plantation dispenses with a middleman, and enables the laborer to make a saving, whereas, if he goes to the hills he makes a loss?—A. Yes, sir. I will put it more definitely: As long as he is under the guidance and care of the proprietor of the plantation he prospers, the planter, as we express it in that country, "loaning him our aid"; we make it very expressive to the negro, we loan him our aid, that is, he must follow our advice, and he has learned to do that, and by doing that he accumulates; but when thrown upon his own resources—there are individual exceptions, of course, where a good many negroes prosper themselves when thrown upon their own resources in Arkansas—but as a general fact, where he leaves the guidance and care of the proprietor of a plantation and subjects himself just as any one else does to the common trading with storekeepers, in a very few years he loses what he has accumulated.

Q. Under these favorable circumstances which surround the laborer on the plantation one would think he ought to accumulate; but I understand you that as a rule he is rather improvident and fails to accumulate. To what do you attribute that improvidence on the part of the negro laborer? —A. It is simply from the want of a proper appreciation of the opportunities of advancement from his condition. The negroes are just beginning, as I expressed it, to realize the responsibilities of life, and just as they begin to realize the responsibilities of life here, they begin to prosper. The prosperity of the South has only begun in the last few years, and it has begun to increase just as the race issue has ceased. I will demonstrate that to you by a little paragraph I cut out of the *New York Herald* last night, taken from the New Orleans *Times-Democrat.* If you take the assessed valuation of real estate in Alabama, in 1879 it was at $117,486,581; in 1883 it is assessed at $152,920,115. There has been that increase in four years from $117,000,000 to $152,000,000. Now let us take the State of Arkansas: in 1879 our real estate was valued at $86,892, 541; in 1883 it is valued at $136,000,000. It goes on just in that same proportion. For instance, this shows that in eight of the Southern and Southwestern States there has been an increase of nearly half a billion dollars—that is, $494,836,686—in value of taxable property during the short period of four years.

I happened to pick up this book last night. If I had an opportunity I could have gotten some statistics to show you the increased production in these different States, and how completely it has taken place, as the laborer has begun to rely on himself and been thrown on his resources.

Q. Have you observed the origin of these statistics?—A. They come from the New Orleans *Times-Democrat.* I will read this in order that they may be known. This is from the *Herald* of yesterday:

SOUTHERN PROGRESS

The New Orleans Times-Democrat has gathered from trustworthy sources and given to the public valuable statistics showing the industrial progress made in the Southern States during the past four years. This covers the period since 1879, the year to which the figures of the latest national census apply. The census returns show a marvelous material growth in the South during the preceding ten years. But, according to the reports published by our New Orleans contemporary, the progress of the past four years is greater and more wonderful than that achieved during the decade between the census years.

Taking the important item of assessed value of property, a comparison between the years 1879 and 1883 gives the following remarkable results:

States	Assessment 1883	Tax rate	Assessment 1879	Tax rate
Alabama	$152,920,115	6½	$117,486,581	7
Arkansas	136,000,000	7	86,892,541	6½
Florida	56,000,000	5	29,471,648	7
Georgia	300,000,000	2½	135,659,530	5
Louisiana	200,000,000	6	209,361,402	6
Mississippi	116,288,810	2½	129,308,345	3½
Tennessee	252,289,873	2	223,211,345	1
Texas	500,000,000	3	304,470,736	5
Total	1,710,498,798	4½	1,215,662,128	5

This shows that in eight Southern and Southwestern States there has been an increase of nearly half a billion dollars—$494,836,668—in the value of taxable property during the short period of four years, while the rate of taxation has been actually reduced. At the same time liberal appropriations have been made for schools, public improvements, and other useful purposes. "Nor is this marvelous advance in valuation," says the *Times-Democrat*, "the result of any inflation in value, but the natural sequence of grand crops, new industries developed, new manufactories, mines, and lumber mills established."

The extension of railroads has been hardly less astonishing. In the eight States above enumerated there were in 1879 11,604 miles of railroad. There are now 17,891 miles, showing an increase in four years of 6,287 miles. The agricultural progress made is shown by the fact that the value of raw products raised in these States, including all crops, lumber, cattle, and wool, has advanced from $398,000,000 in 1879 to $567,000,000 in 1883, or an increase of $169,000,000. During this period the mineral output of Alabama alone has increased from $4,000,000 to $19,000,000, and the lumber product of Arkansa from $1,790,000 to $8,000,000.

The trade of New Orleans is a barometer of Southern industry and commerce. The value of domestic produce in that city in 1881-82 was $159,000,-000; in 1882-83 it was $200,000,000. The value of exports of domestic produce to foreign countries in the former year amounted to $68,000,000; in the latter it reached $95,000,000.

These figures tell a remarkable story of recent progress in the Southern States. Always rich in natural resources, the South has long been poor through lack of development. It has at last entered upon a new era of industrial activity, and is now making rapid strides toward a stage of material prosperity commensurate with its great natural wealth.—*New York Herald*, September 12, 1883.

Now, here is quite a remarkable fact to which I wish to call your attention, to show you the opportunities for labor existing in the South and what is the condition of certain counties in the South. I hold in my hand a book that is compiled for the benefit of the Georgia Pacific Railroad, but I happened to find it in my room and thought these matters would be interesting.

Q. The data you consider reliable?—A. What I read I think comes from the census report; I think this is reliable:

In this connection let us glance at Montgomery County, Alabama, which, although not in the belt we are studying, is on the same prairie formation crossed by the Georgia Pacific Railway, on the edge of Mississippi. Compare it with Butler County, Ohio, which "shows the best record of any county in the West." In live stock Montgomery has $1,748,273; Butler, $1,333,592.

That is the largest producing county in Ohio as compared with Montgomery County, Alabama, before the war.

Montgomery had 63,134 hogs; Butler, 51,640. Animals slaughtered: Montgomery, $336,915; Butler, $318,274. In grain Butler was considerably ahead, but in roots Montgomery led. Montgomery doubled Butler in the production of wool, and had its cotton crop to show besides. The total value of the crops of Montgomery County was $3,264,170; those of Butler only $1,671,132.

There is Montgomery County, Alabama, compared with the leading producing county in Ohio.

Q. Do you know as to the relative size of the two counties?—A. I think it was given here:

A handsome triumph for the Alabama county! And yet Montgomery is not up to the average of the prairie counties of Alabama.

I do not know the relative size. Here is a fact to which I wish to call particular attention:

We have examined the mortality tables of the United States census for 1880, and find that as regards health, Georgia, Alabama, and Mississippi make a better showing than some of the oldest and most densely populated Northern States.

There is generally an idea prevailing that the Southern States are very unhealthy. It is a point that bears directly on our labor question, and for that reason I wish to call special attention to this table, which is taken directly from the census:

ANNUAL DEATH RATE FOR EACH THOUSAND OF POPULATION

New York	17.38
Pennsylvania	14.92
Virginia	16.32
Massachusetts	18.59
Kentucky	14.39
Georgia	13.97
Alabama	14.20
Mississippi	12.89

Mississippi has the smallest average death rate of any of that number of States which I have enumerated.

Q. I suppose the circumstance that the average death rate is larger in cities ought to be taken into account, the Southern population being mostly rural, is it not?—A. The Southern population is to a very great extent rural—Still there are cities in Georgia which I suppose in proportion to our rural population would not make the latter in excess of what it is here. If you take your rural population here and in New Jersey, where you are densely populated, we are no more densely populated in the proportion of our city population to the country than you are here, I think.

Q. Of the population, which is, as a rule, the more healthy in the South, the colored or the white population?

By Mr. PUGH:

Q. There must be some qualification of that difference between the death rate between such States as Massachusetts, for instance, and Georgia, on account of the fact—which I suppose must be conceded—that in these new States population is younger and more vigorous than in the older States. The emigration to these States has been of the younger and more vigorous population, not so liable to die as those who remain behind and are older?—A. There has been but very little emigration into these States up to this census.

Mr. PUGH. That is the fact to some extent, I suppose, anyway.

The CHAIRMAN. In that same connection, I suppose, should be borne in mind the fact that the population of these Eastern States is largely reenforced by immigration from Europe, and that is of the younger and more vigorous European population, and I do not know but what the people in Massachusetts will insist upon it that they are as young and as vigorous as anybody.

Mr. PUGH. I have no doubt. I saw a great many very old people there.

The WITNESS. I merely mentioned this because I wanted to do away with the impression which generally exists that the Southern States are very unhealthy.

Mr. PUGH. I have no doubt that what you state is true as a general fact.

The WITNESS. Now, to bear out the assertion which I made that the prosperity of the negroes began to increase with the cessation of race issues in the South, which has been so apparent to me that I can almost mark the time that it began, look at the cotton crop that is being made to a great extent by small farmers; look at the increase of the cotton crop in the different States in the last few years. For instance, take Georgia: in 1870 she made 473,934 bales of cotton; in 1880 she made 814,441, an increase of 75 per cent. Alabama in 1870 produced 429,482 bales; and in 1880 699,654, an increase of 62 per cent. Mississippi in 1870 produced 564,938 bales; in 1880 she produced 955,808 bales, an increase of 69 per cent.

Here is a very significant fact also with regard to the condition of our laborers in the South, and it shows one of the disadvantages we have had to labor under. During the war, and from the results of the war, nearly all of our live stock was destroyed, a great portion of it was destroyed, which left us after the war without the means of raising our own meat and such supplies at home, and took away from the South a great portion of our wealth, for we know that cattle, hogs &c., increase in arithmetical progress. If you have a hog, this year she bears so many pigs, and in a couple of years those pigs bear so many, and so on. But we were left without live stock. I have here a table which shows, even under those difficulties, the increase in that respect in the Southern States of live stock. These are very significant figures. It is entirely an accident that I happened to get hold of them last night. The live stock of New York in 1870 was 5,286,421; in 1880, 5,422,238, an increase of 2 per cent. In Pennsylvania it was 4,484,748 in 1870; in 1880, 5,255,204, an increase of 17 per cent. In Georgia, in 1870, it was 2,275,137; in 1880, 3,139,101, an increase of 38 per cent. In Alabama it was 1,606,299 in 1870, and in 1880, 2,586,221, an increase of 61 per cent, and in Mississippi, in 1870, it was 1,724,295, and in 1880, 2,398,334, an increase of 38 per cent. This shows that with all the disadvantages the South had to contend with of their stock cattle being destroyed, the natural advantages of climate and pasturage, to which I attribute it, existing in the South have enabled them to increase more rapidly their live stock than any other of the States of the Union. That shows clearly the advantages which that country offers for immigration and labor. This is an advantage to labor. As I stated in my written reply to your submitted questions, we work but few white laborers in my section of the country. Why? Because they soon become land-owners with the opportunities which present themselves to them. The white men will not be there more than two or three years before he has bought and paid for his land in almost every instance.

By the CHAIRMAN:

Q. And he becomes an employer himself?—A. He becomes an employer himself.

Q. Does he usually locate upon the plantation lands along the rivers? —A. No, sir; he cannot buy this land, because the planter would not divide a large plantation into tracts; he would not sell off a portion of his land without selling the whole.

Q. In how large tracts are the plantations held? Just mention the acreage of some of them that you are acquainted with.—A. I would say variously from 500 to 2,500 acres in cultivation.

Q. How valuable are these plantations per acre?—A. That is a question which cannot be answered definitely except in this way: where a planter owns the land, and he is out of debt, the land is not for sale, because he cannot invest his money in anything that is so profitable; but where a planter's proporty is mortgaged, and the mortgagee wants to foreclose and will foreclose, and there is not in that country the money which the planter can borrow to relieve himself of his indebtedness, he will probably sell his land at a small excess of his debt in order to save something. You see there is a want of capital in that country, and if a planter is involved, as many planters are and have been ever since the war, he must do the best he can. There are many planters in that country who are nothing but agents of the factors, from the fact that the interest and commissions they pay upon the debt amount to more than the rent for the property, and they hold on to it as a home. Therefore, a planter in that condition will sell at a nominal price, whereas a plantation owned and paid for is not for sale.

By Mr. PUGH:

Q. There is really no established market price?—A. None at all, owing to the necessity of the one to sell and the desire of another to buy.

By the CHAIRMAN:

Q. At what rates per acre have you known the title to change in some instances?—A. I have known lands to be bought there, including woodlands and cleared lands, at from $20 to $25 an acre, which would be, say, $40 or $50 an acre for the cleared land, and I have known other planters to refuse $80 an acre, cash.

Q. Do you think that $80 or $100 per acre would be a reasonable price for these plantation lands?—A. They sold before the war for $120 an acre.

By Mr. CALL:

Q. You are speaking now of the alluvial lands?—A. I am speaking of the alluvial lands on the Mississippi River, cleared, ready for cultivation, with the improvements existing upon them.

By the CHAIRMAN:

Q. Improved plantations?—A. Yes, sir.

Q. Upon what price per acre do you think those lands would pay, one year with another, an interest of 6 per cent?—A. I will best answer that question by the figures of rents which I have given. The rent, without any responsibility attached to the proprietor at all, is from $8 to $10 an acre.

Q. In money?—A. In money. I will say further that I have been living in that country since 1869, and I have never yet known a year when there has not been a sufficient crop made to pay the rent, without a single exception.

By Mr. CALL:

Q. What is left to the tenant after he pays this $10 an acre?—A. That land produces on an average 400 pounds of lint cotton to the acre, which at 10 cents a pound is $40.

By the CHAIRMAN:

Q. To what extent is Northern capital availing itself of opportunity to invest in these plantations?—A. I might say it is limited.

Q. From what fact does that arise?—A. From the fact that the safety of investments there is just becoming apparent to capitalists. Capitalists up to this time have been afraid to go to the South, owing to the disturbed condition of affairs politically and this very race-issue question. A man does not want to carry his money down there and put it into a country that might be involved in riots and disturbances. Those questions are now just beginning to settle themselves, and capital is beginning to find its way.

Q. Do you anticipate in the near or remote future any further difficulty from the race question?—A. Not at all, and if we are left to ourselves things will very soon equalize themselves.

Q. You are left to yourselves now, are you not?—A. We are now.

Q. All you ask is to continue to be let alone?—A. Just to be let alone. The South, with her natural resources and advantages of climate and soil, feels that she is perfectly able to take care of herself and her affairs, and all she wants is that the legislation of the country, both Federal and State, should be that which will mete out justice to all her citizens, colored as well as white.

Q. Does the South feel as though all she had got to do was to take care of herself, or does she feel a little responsibility for the other section of the country?—A. She feels, more immediately now, responsibility for that section, for this reason, that the negro population of the South, compared with the white population of the South, might be a dangerous element, but the negro population, compared with the whole white population of the United States as an integral body, sinks into insignificance. Therefore, the forces which are at work in the South to-day make us strongly Union. They are directly contrary to what were existing before the war, and there are no people in this Government to-day who have the same interest in the Federal Union that the people of the Southern States have, and they appreciate it.

Q. You feel that it is to your advantage that the negro population should be dealt with by the forty or fifty millions of whites, that the races should be balanced in that proportion rather than in the proportion that exists between them and the white population of the South alone?—A. Yes, sir.

Q. The central idea of the South is a national idea, then?—A. The central idea of the South is more a national idea now than it has been in this respect.

Q. I would use the word "leading" rather than "central" there—the leading idea?—A. We, of course, claim that we want to manage the internal affairs of our States just as much as New York, or New Hampshire, or Massachusetts would want to manage theirs, but that it is necessary for us to have the guidance and protection of the Government: we want it just as much as either of those States.

Q. Have you traveled considerably through the North?—A. I have.

Q. What portions of the North have you visited within the last few years?—A. I have visited Philadelphia, New York, Boston, Hartford, and I might say a number of other points in the States of which they are the chief cities.

Q. While we are speaking of this matter of reciprocal feeling between the sections of country, as you have mentioned the attitude of the South, I should like to know from you, from your personal observation and knowledge, what you find to be that of the North toward the South?—A. I think it is of the kindliest character. I have never in my life been treated with more consideration than I have been by gentlemen in the East who were most opposed to the South during the war.

Q. I do not refer simply to personal courtesy, but I mean the expression of feeling as between the sections, the general tendency and drift of Northern feeling towards the Southern portions of the country, to the people of the South?—A. I think, so far as I have been able to observe, that the feeling in the East towards the South is a general anxiety for her prosperity. I would go so far as to speak of it as anxiety for her prosperity.

Q. You think the war of sections is pretty much over?—A. I think it is obliterated, and for that reason I go back to this point, that our prosperity in the South has begun.

Q. You have described with some minuteness the condition of things among the planters and those who work upon the plantations. I should like to ask this question further, whether any of the negroes along the alluvial bottoms are obtaining ownership of lands in fee-simple?—A. In very few instances in the alluvial lands. When they make enough money to buy a home they generally go to the hill country, where land can be bought at a much more reasonable price.

Q. With what amount of accumulation will a negro get up and go to the hills?—A. There are negroes right in my section of the country who have an accumulation clear of all expenses of from a thousand to $3,500 a year.

Q. Do they remain or do they go and buy homesteads for themselves? —A. They probably remain until they accumulate a few thousand dollars, and then go and buy a home. We encourage it, from the fact that we want the others behind to be stimulated to do the same thing. I will say in that connection that the future of the negro of the South is the alluvial lands.

Q. These plantations?—A. Not only these plantations particularly. What I mean by alluvial lands are the alluvial lands on the coast and the alluvial lands of the Mississippi Valley, the rich lands where the negro relies on his own energy and exertion rather than on his brains. There is an immigration coming into the older States now.

Q. The older Southern States?—A. The older Southern States. As they come in the negroes gradually give way and go to the richer lands. For instance, one railroad last year brought into the Mississippi Valley over 10,000 negro immigrants.

Q. From what States?—A. From the Atlantic and Gulf States.

Q. What became of them?—A. They were scattered along the alluvial lands of the Mississippi Valley. As the negroes of the Mississippi Valley either immigrate from that valley and go in different directions and buy land, the planters of the Mississippi Valley send out to the older States and replace them with labor from those States. A negro in the older States, probably, to make his support would have to cultivate 15 or 20 acres of land, whereas a negro in the Mississippi Valley can make his support on 8 or 10 acres of land.

Q. Will this result in the ownership of the alluvial lands being transferred to the negro?—A. No, sir; because as he makes money he goes off.

Q. He is a Chinese immigrant?—A. I mean by "goes off" he does not go out of the State, but he goes to the hills.

Q. And to smaller ownerships?—A. To smaller ownerships.

Q. And the aim of the Southern planter is to accommodate this tendency of things to smaller rentings?—A. Yes, sir.

Q. Do you think a plantation is more productive where, under a general supervision by the planter or the owner, it is let out in small sections to the negroes to cultivate, or is it better to cultivate the plantation as a whole?—A. It is better to let it out, as I stated in my written answers. The cotton crop of this country is being raised to such an extent by the small white farmers that the large planter can no longer afford to hire and compete with that class of labor who only expend their own energy; consequently the tendency is to make farmers of the negroes.

Q. What chance is there of the planter securing white labor to carry on these plantations?—A. There is such a small proportion of white labor in the South that it would be difficult for him to find them, and the tide of foreign immigration is just beginning to be turned in that direction. There has been a prejudice against white emigrants going to the South, on account of going among the negroes.

Q. Do you think that is diminishing?—A. Diminishing yearly.

Q. You mean that immigration from Europe is being employed on the plantations?—A. Not exactly upon the large cotton plantations, but the smaller plantations are now being converted into farms. For instance, there has been a large immigration of European emigrants into that section of the country between Little Rock and Fort Smith.

Q. Do they, upon these farm or small plantations being converted into farms, work in companionship with the negro laborer?—A. No; they generally buy the land and work it themselves; they may hire a negro and work with him; they are laborers themselves.

Q. Is there any tendency among the white and colored laborers of any class to work in companionship, or to fraternize at all in labor?—A. I cannot say that there is. A white man would not take a negro in as a partner to work with him in the field.

Q. And will a white man find any difficulty in hiring another white man and negro to work together side by side in the field?—A. No, sir; I have them myself working side by side.

Q. There is no prejudice of that kind?—A. None at all.

Q. No white man inquires whether he can work by himself or is to work in company with a negro? Do they exhibit any reluctance to work in company with the negro?—A. The class of white people that work in our country for wages comes from Ohio, and Missouri, and Indiana, and that section of country, and I find there is some prejudice among that class of people sometimes, but still there are instances—as I say, I have men from Indiana now myself hired working right in a gang with negroes.

Q. There is no strong tendency in that way, I suppose?—A. No strong tendency in that way. There are no white laborers from the South proper; at least the number we can hire for wages is so small that it is not sufficient to call it a class.

Q. In the Southern States proper about two thirds of the population is white, is it not?—A. I do not recollect. According to the census returns I think there are about seven millions of negroes. The census would give the exact statement.

Q. Not far from two thirds of the population, I think, is white. In the Gulf States proper at least one half the population must be white. In what way is the white laboring population of the South employed?—A. They are employed as small farmers nearly almost entirely.

Q. Not to as great extent as mechanics and artisans?—A. I suppose there is a liberal proportion of them to the population; we have to have our artisans and mechanics; but as a rule the white population of the South are small farmers, either owners of the land themselves or tenants.

Q. How as to their material prosperity and thrift and saving?—A. It varies very much. For instance, take the State of Georgia—and I believe it is admitted that Georgia is one of the most thrifty and prosperous of all the Southern States—I think the small farmers are generally self-sustaining; they raise their own supplies.

Q. Do these small white farmers employ negro help to any extent?—A. To a certain extent. If a man has more land than his family can work he will hire a negro laborer. There is no prejudice against his doing so either on the part of the farmer hiring him or the negro hired.

Q. He may hire some white and other colored laborers, I suppose?—A. Yes, sir.

Q. Do they work together?—A. Yes, sir.

Q. How in regard to the value of the hill lands you have spoken of in the State of Arkansas; as compared with the alluvial, what is the difference in value?—A. It is very great. There are farms in Arkansas that can be bought, partially cleared up, and with some improvements upon them, for from $5 to $20 an acre, less than the rent of fair lands on the river. There is no finer section of country in the world—I say that unhesitatingly—for a foreign immigrant, or the immigrant from the East, or from anywhere, than is afforded to-day in Arkansas and Texas.

Q. And political disturbances are at an end?—A. We apprehend nothing at all; there is no reason why we should.

Q. You were speaking of the necessity of the education of the laborer of the South, the negro especially. Will you not describe to us the actual condition of the masses of the colored people in the matter of education, to what extent it has progressed, and what facilities and opportunities exist, and what additional are required?—A. It varies in different sections. For instance, Georgia, and Tennessee are probably ahead of any of the Southern States in point of educating the colored people; they have more facilities; they have negro primary schools and colleges where a man is educated. The education that I was speaking of, more particularly for the negro, is a plain English education, sufficient to enable him to read and write.

Q. What we call up North a common school education?—A. A common school education. I will illustrate that. Suppose a negro comes to me to make a contract that I have written for him, and he cannot read or write. I offer that contract to him, and I read it to him. He touches a pen and signs his mark to it; there is no obligation attached at all. He says at once, "That man is an educated man; he has the advantage of me; he shows me that contract; I do not know what is in it; I cannot even read it." Therefore a contract made with a negro in that way is almost a nullity; but if he could read that contract himself and sign his own name to it, it would be a very different thing. I never allow a negro to sign a written contract with me before he has taken it home with him and had some friend to read it over and consult with him about it, because I want some obligation attached to my contracts.

Q. It is necessary for you as well as the negro?—A. Necessary for my protection as well as his.

Q. How many of the negroes on the plantations can comprehend a written contract by reading it, because a man may be somewhat educated and not be able to decipher a contract?—A. I cannot give you an exact proportion, for it varies to a great extent. I can only say that that number is increasing rapidly.

Q. From what circumstances comes this increase?—A. From their desire to gain knowledge.

Q. Do you find that desire strong among the colored people?—A. Very strong indeed; and there are two ideas which a negro possesses that give me great hopes for his future. If I did not believe the negro was capable of sufficient development to make him a responsible small farmer, I should not want to remain in the business that I am any longer, because

I believe that the development of my business is necessarily based upon the development of the negro and the cultivation of my lands. The negro possesses two remarkable qualifications: one is that he is imitative, and the other is that he has got pride; he wants to dress well; he wants to do as well as anybody else does when you get him aroused, and with these two qualifications I have very great hopes for him in the future.

Q. What do you think of his intellectual and moral qualities and his capacity for development?—A. There are individual instances I know of where negroes have received and taken a good education. As a class, it would probably be several generations, at any rate, before they would be able to compete with the Caucasian. I believe that the negro is capable of receiving an ordinary English education, and there are instances where they enter professions and become good lawyers. For instance, I know in the town of Greenville, Miss., right across the river from me, a negro attorney, who is a very intelligent man, and I heard one of the leading attorneys in Greenville say he would almost have anybody on the opposite side of a case rather than he would that negro. The sheriff of my county is from Ohio, and a negro, he is a man whom we all support in his office. We are anxious that the negroes should have a fair representation. For instance, you ask for the feeling existing between the proprietor and the negroes. The probate judge of my county is a negro and one of my tenants, and I am here now in New York attending to important business for my county as an appointee of that man. He has upon him the responsibilities of all estates in the county; he is probate judge.

Q. Is he a capable man?—A. A very capable man, and an excellent, good man, and a very just one.

Q. Do you see any reason why, with fair opportunities assured to himself and to his children, he may not become a useful and competent, American citizen?—A. We already consider him so.

Q. The question is settled?—A. I thought you were speaking personally of the man I referred to.

Q. No; I was speaking of the negro generally—the negro race.—A. Let me understand your question exactly.

Q. Do you see any reason why the negroes, as a component part of the American population, may not, with a fair chance, come to be useful, industrious, and competent to the discharge of the duties of citizenship? —A. I think they may as a class, but it will take probably generations for them to arrive at that standard.

Q. It has taken us generations to arrive at the standard, has it not?— A. Yes, sir.

Q. There is some talk about our ancestors having been pirates, I be-believe. Now, will you state to us what the existing facilities for education are among the negroes?—A. I can only speak as regards Arkansas. Of course I do not know much of the other States. In Arkansas we have in each county a school board. These boards examine and employ teachers. We are taxed for a school fund, from which these teachers are paid.

Q. What proportion of the colored children attend school, do you think?—A. On my own property there are five schools, and I think the larger portion, I might say nearly all that are capable of going to school, do go to school.

Q. How many children are there on your own property?—A. I could scarcely form an idea.

Q. There are five schools?—A. There are five schools, and I should suppose from 300 to 500 children.

Q. Those are educated in public schools?—A. Yes, sir.

Q. I understand you to say that nearly all of them attend?—A. Yes, sir.

Q. For how long a time each year is school kept open?—A. The schools extend all the year except vacation, I think, which is about three months; but a number of the negroes will withdraw their children from school during cotton-picking season, to help them pick the crop.

Q. Between what ages do they actually attend school?—A. From 6 to 19. I know a great many of them who are going to school who are 17, 18, and 19, who can just begin to read and write a little.

Q. Do you find any inclination among the older negroes who are past school age to endeavor to read and write?—A. Not very much, but they are anxious their children should, and appeal to them. In almost every instance where a man has a child who can read and write, he will bring him along with him when he makes a contract. They are very proud of their children being able to read and write.

Q. Are they satisfied, as a rule, with their simply becoming able to read and write, or do they like to have them make a little further progress in mathematics, geography, &c.?—A. As a class they look to them simply to read and write. They think when they have got that far they know everything; but then there are certain ones who have ambition, just as it is with our own race. There are some men who have tastes for literature, and receive a better education than others do, but it is not the same pro-portion of the negro race of course that it is with our own. There are in-stances where negroes are also anxious to obtain a collegiate education, and become school teachers.

Q. I do not know that you are able to state to what extent they actually attend school in the hill districts?—A. I am not.

Q. You speak both of your own plantation and of other plantations as well as your own in that regard?—A. I am speaking of the alluvial lands along the Mississippi River.

Q. In Arkansas?—A. Not only in Arkansas, but in Louisiana and Mississippi; I will say the alluvial lands on the Mississippi River between Memphis and Vicksburg.

Q. Are the negroes on those lands generally having the same opportunities for education that they do on your plantation?—A. Oh, yes, sir; there is a common school system.

Q. And it is as prevalent in Louisiana and Mississippi as in Arkansas? —A. I think it is.

Q. What is the nativity of those teachers, as a rule?—A. They are generally colored people from either the East or the Northwest. There are some white teachers, but very few.

Q. Are any of the white teachers Southern in birth?—A. There is not a white teacher on my own property; they are all colored teachers on my own property. The proportion of white teachers is very small.

Q. How much do these colored teachers themselves know?—A. Some of them are remarkably well educated.

Q. And generally earnestly devoted to their work?—A. Perfectly so.

Q. Or is it simply to get their money?—A. No; I think some of them really have a desire to see their scholars advance.

Q. Some pride in their race, to have them get on, I suppose?—A. I think there is a certain pride in that respect; and, again, they want to gain a reputation as teachers.

Q. What compensation does a teacher get?—A. I think about from $50 to $100 a month.

Q. Do they pay their own expenses, board and shelter?—A. Yes, sir; but board is cheap, merely nominal.

Q. About what amount?—A. I should say these teachers can get board for $10 a month.

Q. Is the cost of clothing in your part of the country about the same as here?—A. This is our market.

Q. You buy the ready-made clothing largely for the population in general, I suppose?—A. We buy both ready-made clothing and cloth to make up.

Q. I suppose the colored population hardly buy custom goods?—A. A great many of them buy the cloth, and some of their women are as good tailoresses as you would find anywhere. They buy the cloth and make it up themselves.

Q. That must bring a suit of clothes pretty cheap in a colored family; they really expend nothing but buy the cloth themselves?—A. They sell very good jeans cloth there at 35 or 40 cents a yard; they generally wear jeans.

Q. All seasons of the year?—A. Generally in all seasons of the year. In the summer time a laboring man hardly ever wears a coat at all.

Q. What do you think an average colored Southern laborer expends per annum for his clothing, say the head of the family, the man—what does it cost him for clothing a year?—A. I cannot give you a definite answer. I will only say that we who are the producers of cotton are very glad to see them get in a prosperous condition in order that there may be more consumption, and when a man is prosperous he will buy two suits of clothes, where if he is not prosperous he will make one do.

Q. We have had a good deal of testimony as to what it actually costs a Northern laborer a year for clothing. I have no desire to show that any laborers dress cheaply or poorly; I merely want to get an idea of the relative cost of the laboring man living North or South, in the item of clothing?—A. I can sell and do sell a man a pair of jeans pants and a coat from $7 to $12 per suit.

Q. How many suits will he want in a year?—A. That will depend on his condition and his ability to pay me. If he is a prosperous man and beginning to accumulate he will make one do. Whenever a negro begins to accumulate he goes to extremes; he does not want to buy anything; he wants to accumulate rapidly. Where a man is not doing so well, and there is little doubt of his ability to pay, he would probably want several suits; but I would confine him to one or two.

Q. The same is true, I suppose, of his wife and children?—A. Yes, sir.

Q. But you look on the matter of clothing as a much less expensive item in the laborer's account in your country than here in the North where the climate is colder, I suppose?—A. Yes, sir. What absorbs the profit of the laborers with us is their want of providence; that is, if they get surplus money they throw it away for useless articles.

Q. It has been suggested that a postal savings bank might be a good thing as a place of deposit of the savings of the colored population of the South; they might feel some confidence in an institution of that kind, and that it would be a beneficial thing to them. What is your own judgment?—A. I advocate it and approve it, and indeed propose to start a savings bank in our own neighborhood. In this connection I will mention another important feature. In the Mississippi Valley—and when I speak of the Mississippi Valley I mean both sides of the river, Arkansas and Louisiana on one side and Mississippi on the other—there are numbers of negroes who have considerable accumulations and use their surplus to advance to other negroes. For instance, there are negroes right on our property who have accumulated enough to help out certain others, as they express it, and they use their money as an investment in that way. For instance one negro who has got something will advance it to another negro and take a mortgage on his crop. Consequently there are numbers of them who are getting advances from their co-laborers, and I always give them that opportunity when they want it. My idea of the adjustment in the Mississippi Valley, seeing what I can make from the mercantile portion of my business, is that it is simply my revenue that I get from the rent of my land as an investment on my capital; and whenever a negro can get his own merchant in New Orleans—a number of them have very good factors in New Orleans and ship their cotton direct—I encourage it. When one negro wants to help out another, I give him the privilege of doing it and encourage it. There are several negroes, a great many, not a few in Chicot County to-day who have their own factors in New Orleans, ship their own goods, and receive their own accounts of sales.

Q. They are not owners of alluvial lands?—A. They are not owners at all; they are tenants.

Q. I suppose some time they will be liable to make some accumulations, and they will now and then own a plantation?—A. I do know of one instance on the river below Vicksburg where the old property of Mr. Davis was bought by a former slave of his.

Q. Is that the only instance?—A. The only instance I know of.

Q. One question we have been accustomed to put is as to the actual personal feeling that exists between the laborers and capitalists of different parts of the country. What is the feeling between the laborers, colored and white, and the owners of the land and of capital at the South?—A. I confine my replies to my own section, because I am not familiar with the others. I have answered that question in the written answers. The feeling is harmonious and good, as I have expressed it there. The negro naturally looks to the planter for advice and for assistance, and the planter looks to his laborers for the development of his property. Consequently their interests are identical and their feelings good.

Q. You have alluded once or twice to the pressure of outside, and I suppose Northern, opinion; I assume that you mean political opinion in the past and the desirability that it should cease. What is the fact as to a

progressive disintegration of the solid Republican or solid negro vote of
the South? What are the chances of its dividing, and of the white vote
dividing? We hear now of a "solid South," colored on the one side and
white on the other. What prospect is there of a division in that regard; to
what extent does it exist, or is it going on?—A. The negroes of the South
are already divided in their votes. There are a great many who vote with
the proprietors of the properties. There are instances where they vote with
what they call their Republican friends. A few years ago in the South any
man who was an escaped convict from one of your penitentiaries here
who would come down to that country and tell the negroes that he was one
of General Grant's soldiers, and fought to free him, would vote the last
one out; but any of those negroes would come to me at that very time
with his money and get me to save it for him, and take care of it for him.
He would put all his confidence in me so far as his money was concerned,
but when it would come to politics he would vote with this man, who
probably did not own the coat he had on his back. Those kind of inferences were what did do us in the South very material damage. Let me
illustrate that by a riot in my own county. In Chicot County, in 1872,
there was a proposition to impose upon the county a railroad tax of $250,-
000 for the purpose of building a railroad.

Q. What proportion of the taxable property of the county would that
have been?—A. Our whole assessed valuation was about $1,500,000 at
that time. This was brought out by a promise that if the appropriation
was made, the levees on our river should be built and this road would run
on the levees. At that time the whole of the local government in Chicot
County was in the hands of men who did not own any property in the
county, and had just come down there and been elected by the negroes,
who have a very large majority in that county. This tax was a very great
imposition upon us. At that time there was a negro attorney at Lake
Village, who was one of the prime movers in this thing. The planters knew
that this was only intended as a speculation upon the county, for the vote
was afterwards taken, the appropriation was made, and not one foot of
levee was put up, and not one foot of that railroad was built in Chicot
County. Still we are mandamused now for the interest on that debt that
was put on us by that kind of influence. One of our planters was remon-
strating with this negro attorney about this debt and told him it was an
imposition on the property owners, and that the thing ought not to be
done, when the man became violent and insolent, and it resulted in a
difficulty between this planter and the negro. The planter had a little
pen-knife in his pocket, the blade not longer than my little finger; he

struck the negro with it and it happened accidentally to hit him on a vital point and killed him. The sheriff of the county was a negro. The planter, with two innocent parties in whose house this occurrence took place at the county-seat, in Lake Village, was arrested and lodged in jail. A few days afterwards—probably not more than two or three—nearly every negro in the county was summoned to Lake Village, and they rose like so many locusts, coming in from every direction, took those three men out of jail shot them to pieces, murdered them. It was such an outrage that the people from Memphis and Vicksburg and from the hill countries, commenced to come in there with companies, started down with companies. On investigation we found out that the sheriff of the county had exercised his authority to send out to the ignorant negroes of the county and summon them to the village, and these fellows went because they were afraid not to obey the mandate of the sheriff. At that time feeling was running very high, and these people were anxious to come in and quell this riot, but a few of us who were more prudent, a few of the leading planters of the county, got together, sent these different companies word not to come there, that we did not want them in the county; some of the companies were already on their way to Chicot County, thinking the people there were going to be massacred. A great many of our people had to run away from their homes for several days; but we took the ground that we would let the thing take its natural course. As soon as things quieted down, which they did so partially in three or four days, some of our gentlemen who had gone off with their families returned, and it resulted in our arresting a few of the ringleaders in the county. The courts and the administration were all at that time in the hands of persons not identified with the interests of the county, and it was impossible for us to get justice meted out. We saved a massacre of the negroes of the county, but we never could bring those men to any kind of punishment before the courts, and finally we came to a compromise with them, that if they would leave the county we would withdraw the suit against them, and that was the way the thing was ended. Now, I do not believe you could get up a riot in Chicot County because I think there are many intelligent negroes there who would not permit it. Those are the kind of race issues that I referred to. Relieve us of that sort of thing, and leave our government to ourselves and our people, and give to the negro the same protection the white man has, but do not give him any more. Do not let him feel that he has the United States Government standing behind him, and that he is the child of the United States Government to be taken care of, but that he must rely on his own resources and energy for his living, and time will solve the question, and the demand for his labor will protect him.

Q. Do you find that the feeling among the negroes which resulted in the exodus of a few years ago has been allayed and perhaps has disappeared?—A. I will tell you something that is rather amusing about that. The first that I heard of a negro exodus in my section of the country—it was to Kansas—was my manager coming into my room one morning and saying that the negroes were going out to the river to go to Kansas. I said, "It is several miles to the river; how are they going?" Said he, "They are toting their things out on their heads." Said I, "Go right at once there and offer them the wagons on the plantation to haul the things. What is the matter?" Said he, "I don't know; I went out this morning and summoned the hands to the field, but they say they are all going to Kansas." I got on my horse and rode out and met a negro who had been my engineer. I said to him, "What is the matter, where are you all going?" He stopped right on the road and said, "Mr. Calhoun, you never have deceived me, and I am going to tell you what is the matter. There were two men came through here last week, one night, and said 'You see this picture?' There is a picture of a farm in Kansas for me that General Grant has bought out there for me. That is so because my name is on the back of it, and here is my ticket; that carries me to Kansas." Said I, "Let me see it." He showed me a piece of pasteboard that had printed on it "Good for one trip to Kansas." Said I, "What did you pay him for this?" He said, "We paid him $2 a piece." "How many of you are in this thing?" "Over eighty of us are in this thing." Said I, "That man then swindled you out of $160; he is an imposter; there is no farm bought for you in Kansas." I saw that the time for me to remonstrate with them was not then; they were on their way to the Mississippi River, and I let them all go. After they got out there I went and expostulated with them; told them of the difference in climate, soil, and everything else that they were accustomed to, and that if they went there many of them would lose their families and children. They would not listen to me. They went on to the river bank, and those negroes who went out there owed me over $109,000.

Q. How many of them were there? Eighty I think you said?—A. There were 80, I think. Once, I suppose, there were 150 negroes, perhaps more, on the bank of the river. They were not at a regular landing. They went out to the intermediate points where a boat would not be compelled to land. We notified all the boats coming up the river not to land at this point. I did not want these negroes to go off, being satisfied that they were going to their ruin if they did; that they were leaving comfortable homes; many of them had sold their mules or given them away at a mere sacrifice. One negro sold a mule worth $150 for $15 to get off. They opened their potato-houses, they opened their corn-cribs and scattered the corn, giving it away to everybody that would offer them five cents a bushel. I had given two of these people a piece of land, the productions of all of which they were to have for bringing it into cultivation and improving it. Knowing the negro nature as I do, and knowing that he would not want anybody to derive the benefit of something that he thought he was entitled to, I got two white men in the county to come and offer me to take this piece of land and cultivate it on shares with me, giving me one half its product, whereas with them I was entitled to nothing. As soon as those two fellows found out that I had made a good bargain for their land they went back home from the river bank, and as soon as they went back all the rest followed. Then I called the whole plantation up and told them to appoint two representatives and that I would send them to Kansas at my own expense to examine into this matter and report to them. These two men went to Kansas, came back, and reported the true condition of affairs; and now if what they call in that country "a poor white man"—the negro's expression—goes through the country and says "Kansas," they almost want to mob him. That was the result of the Kansas movement.

Q. What has become of those who went to Kansas?—A. Many of them have returned and many have died; numbers of them have died. Quite a large number went to Washington County Mississippi, just opposite me.

Q. From time to time, at Washington, efforts are being made to secure public lands in the Territories, the Indian Territory and elsewhere, for the purpose of colonizing such tracts with negroes. Do you think there is any sort of occasion for that?—A. None in the world. If the alluvial lands on the Mississippi River were protected from overflow and brought into a condition where they could be cultivated they would afford all the homes, and of the best character, that the negroes could possibly want in the South, and the natural tendency is to come to just such lands.

Q. And the negroes prefer to be there to anywhere else?—A. Those that come, I notice, never go back.

Q. You suggested the improvement of the levees. What is the necessity, and in what degree is it difficult for those residing along the river banks to protect themselves?—A. I am the president of the levee board of Chicot County. The plan which has been suggested by the Mississippi River Commission and Mr. Eads, as their chief engineer, is unquestionably the correct one for the improvement of the Mississippi River. We know this not only from theory, but from long experience with the river, those of us who have lived there. The Mississippi River being, as it is generally termed, the "Father of Waters," and passing through several States, it is almost a national system, and it would be impossible for any system to be adopted by the States which would be local. Consequently it is imperatively the duty of the Government of the United States to take care of the improvement of the Mississippi River. There are certain sections of the Mississippi River that are naturally above overflow, made so by cutoffs. The fall of the Mississippi River is about four inches to the mile. Consequently, when there is one of those large bends, where the river runs around where the cut-off is, no increase of water is needed. The fall being four inches to the mile, the lands just above the cut-off are made higher and above overflow, whereas just below, the lands are overflowed or become liable to overflow. The improvement of the Mississippi River itself for commercial purposes, as well as the protection of the lands, is dependent upon the building of the levees, for the levees of course confine the water within its banks, and give not only a greater volumn of water, but greater velocity for scouring purposes, which seours out the sand bars that are formed continually on the river. Captain Eads's plan of forming jetties where the banks cave, saves this deposit, as it were, in the water, which makes the sand bars. A mattress is put against the caving banks which prevents the alluvial land caving into the river which forms the sand bars below. Then the increased volumn and increased velocity of the water wash out the channel, and improve it for commercial purposes, answering the object of protecting the land, and at the same time opening that immense channel for commerce.

Again, there are very important lines of railroad that are being built up and down either bank of the Mississippi River, and it is necessary they should be protected for commercial purposes, as well as that the Mississippi River should be improved for commercial purposes, and they can only be protected by the building of levees. We who have been on the river, and who feel that we are familiar with it, have closely watched the course of the Commission, and I can only say, as an expression of the opinion of the people, that we indorse what the Commission are doing.

Q. And desire still more of it?—A. Yes, sir; it is absolutely necessary. What has already been expended by the Government would be absolutely useless unless additional appropriations are made to complete the work. I would like to call your attention to this point. The Atchafalaya, in Louisiana, is a stream which runs from just about the mouth of Red River into the Gulf of Mexico. The fall from the mouth of the Atchafalaya and

Red River to the Gulf of Mexico is very much greater than the fall from the mouth of Red River to the Gulf by way of New Orleans down the Mississippi River. A few years ago the Atchafalaya was a stream which could be waded across, but owing to the current gradually going through it, it commenced to wash out until now it has got to be a stream 100 feet deep.

Q. Is there or not any perceptible increase or diminution of the column of the Mississippi itself as compared with 25, or 50, or 100 years ago?—A. We think that our waters are higher now than they have ever been before.

Q. Greater extremes, or is there a uniform flow?—A. A larger uniform flow, and it is attributed to the destruction of the forests, though that is mere theory. One of the arguments, at any rate, is that it is owing to the destruction of the forests in the Northwest, which causes more rain storms and gives a larger rainfall.

Q. I have heard the idea advanced that the destruction of the woods and timber about the headwaters would, in case of rain, lead to a more rapid deposit in the stream, it would not be held back by the swampy nature of the soil, and so you might have more sudden rises and falls in the river than formerly without the volume of water or the uniform flow being increased or lessened?—A. I think—at least I have heard it so expressed by men experienced on the river—that the flow of the Mississippi River is greater now than it was formerly.

Q. That one year with another, more water runs down the channel? —A. We can see a slight increase of the water of the Mississippi River. I do not know how it may increase in the future, or if it will at all, but that is the opinion of people there now. The point I want to call your attention to specifically is the necessity for the prevention of the water of the Red River going down through the Atchafalaya, for if the Atchafalaya washes out it leaves New Orleans, a large commercial city, upon, as it were, an inland sea. The waters which overflow from the banks of the Mississippi River on the front of Arkansas go over into the Red River and never come back into the Mississippi River any more until they come out at the mouth of the Red River. Just at the mouth of Red River, and before Red River reaches the Mississippi, is the Atchafalaya. So that all of this overflow water that could be kept in the Mississippi River by building the levees on the front of Arkansas, now goes into Red River and helps to wash out the Atchafalaya, which will ruin the city of New Orleans if that is not prevented. It is a very strong commercial point, for the commerce of New Orleans is a matter to be considered in our affairs.

Q. I suppose there is no doubt that the Atchafalaya furnishes an outlet, which relieves your plantations very much?—A. No, sir; it does not affect where I live at all.

Q. Below the Red River, in Louisiana, is it not a relief in case of an overflow?—A. A partial relief; but in Louisiana, when you get down that far, they pretty much have their system of levees built, which protect the sugar district; there are only probably a few gaps; and the Mississippi River, when it gets that far down, does not rise in the same proportion that it does where I live, 500 miles above. The mouth of the Atchafalaya is 500 miles below where I am.

Q. Has this increased drainage from the Atchafalaya resulted in any injury to the navigation of the river as far north?—A. Not as yet; but if it is not stopped—the commission realize the fact I am now telling you— if it is not checked, the whole Mississippi River will naturally turn through the Atchafalaya, because the fall is so much greater.

Q. How do they propose to check it?—A. That is a matter the commission and scientific engineers would have to decide.

Q. Can they block it at the outlet of the Red River?—A. They propose to check it principally by stopping the water from the Mississippi River that goes into the Red River. There would in that way be an enormous quantity of water kept out of Red River. That would be one method. What the engineers would consider sufficient or necessary to be done, of course I would not venture to express an opinion upon.

Q. What danger is there to the large mass of capital invested in these alluvial lands, unless something is done to prevent the overflows of which you speak?—A. The lands that are now liable to overflow are almost entirely abandoned.

Q. To how large an extent are they now abandoned?—A. Taking in the whole of Mississippi Valley proper, from Memphis down.

Q. Has there been any computation or reasonable estimate that you know of the value of those lands affected by the overflow?—A. I have never heard of it; but I will say that those lands which are liable to overflow now, if brought into cultivation, are just as valuable as any we are cultivating; probably more so, because they have the alluvial deposits upon them. There is a deposit there from 3 to 4 inches.

Q. You have no idea of the extent of those lands?—A. I cannot give you the proportion. I will simply say it is a very large proportion.

Q. A third, or a half, or a quarter?—A. More than a half. I saw it estimated some time ago, at least I will give it as a statement published in the *Planters' Journal,* published in Vicksburgh, that there are thirteen counties on the Mississippi River which, if all cleared up and put into cultivation, are capable of producing the entire cotton crop of the United States, and I have heard the question discussed.

Q. What prevents their being cleared up and put into cultivation?—A. Simply the overflow.

Q. Have they ever been cleared as yet?—A. A great portion of them; and now destroyed because the levee system is not complete. On these lands all the negro labor which is not found profitable on the poorer lands in the older States, could be made extremely profitable, not only to the proprietors of the lands, but to the laborers themselves.

Q. Do you think it would be within limit to say that one half of the alluvial plantation lands, such as you have described in Arkansas, Mississippi, and Louisiana, is now practically destroyed by reason of this overflow occasioned by the destruction of the levee system?—A. Yes, sir.

Q. At least one half?—A. At least one half of that which has been in cultivation, and which can be brought into cultivation.

Q. Of that which is thus useless now, what portion has been formerly under cultivation?—A. It would be impossible for any one to form an estimate, because it is so varied.

Q. The amount of land that has been improved and which is now destroyed by reason of the overflow, you cannot state?—A. I cannot state it accurately; I will state it approximately; I should say at least one third.

Q. One third of the entire amount that has been improved is now destroyed by reason of the overflow, resulting from imperfections in the levee system?—A. Yes, sir; that is what I mean to say.

Q. And of that which has not been improved but might be improved, how much?—A. At least half.

As I have devoted some space to the general condition of labor in the whole country, and as some of my statements and conclusions may be looked upon as extravagant, I deem it very pertinent to add to the appendix a portion of the testimony of Dr. R. Heber Newton, given before Senator Blair's Committee on the *"Relations between Capital and Labor,"* in New York City, September 18, 1883 (Vol. II., p. 535). Dr. Newton is recognized as a clear thinker and a ready writer not only on theological but on economic questions as well. His testimony on the points to which I have asked attention was as follows:

A LABOR QUESTION COMING

The broad fact that the United States census of 1870 estimated the average annual income of our wage-workers at a little over $400 per capita, and that the census of 1880 estimates it at a little over $300 per capita, is the quite sufficient evidence that there is a labor question coming upon us in this country. The average wages of 1870 indicated, after due allowance for the inclusion of women and children, a mass of miserably paid labor—that is, of impoverished and degraded labor. The average wages of 1880 indicated that this mass of semi-pauperized labor is rapidly increasing, and that its condition has become 25 per cent worse in ten years. The shadow of the old-world *proletariat* is thus seen to be stealing upon our shores. It is for specialists in political economy to study this problem in the light of the large social forces that are working such an alarming change in our American society. In the consensus of their ripened judgment we must look for the authoritative solution of this problem. I am not here to assume that rôle. I have no pet hobby to propose, warranted to solve the whole problem without failure. I do not believe there is any such specific yet out. * * *

I

THE FAULTS OF LABOR

Plainly, labor's fault must be found with itself.

1. Leaving upon one side the class of skilled labor, a large proportion of our wage-workers are notoriously inefficient. In the most common tasks one has to watch the average workingman in order to prevent his bungling a job. Hands are worth little without some brains; as in the work done, so in the pay won. Our labor is quite as largely uninterested—having no more heart than brains back of the hands. Work is done mechanically by most workingmen, with little pride in doing it well, and little ambition to be continually doing it better.

2. There is too commonly as little sense of identity with the employer's interests, or of concern that any equivalent in work should be rendered for the pay received. In forms irritating beyond expression employers are made to feel that their employees do not in the least mind wasting their material, injuring their property, and blocking their business in the most critical moments. Under what possible system, save in a grievous dearth of

laborers, can such labor be well off, and incompetence and indifference draw high wages?

3. Our labor is for the most part very thriftless. In the purchase and in the preparation of food—the chief item of expense in the workingman's family and that wherein economic habits count for most—men and women are alike improvident. The art of making money go the farthest in food is comparatively unknown. Workingmen will turn up their noses at the fare on which a Carlyle did some of the finest literary work of our century. I remember some time ago speaking to one of our butchers, who told me that workingmen largely ordered some of his best cuts. Now an ample supply of nutritious food is certainly essential for good work, whether of the brain or of the brawn. The advance of labor is rightly gauged, among other ways, by its increasing consumption of wheat and meat, but the nutritiousness of meat is not necessarily dependent upon its being from the finest cut. I should like to see all men eating "French" chops and porter-house steaks if they could afford it; but when I know the average wages of our workingmen and the cost of living on the simplest possible scale, it is discouraging to learn such a fact as that which I have mentioned, since all the elements of necessary sustenance can be had in so much cheaper forms. * * *

4. Labor must fault itself further, on the ground of its lack of power of combination and of its defective methods in combination. It has been by combination that the middle class has arisen, and by it that capital has so wonderfully increased. The story of the Middle Ages, familiar to us all, is the story of the rise of the industrial class by combination in guilds. Labor's numbers, now a hindrance, might thus become a help. In a mob men trample upon each other; in an army they brace each other to the charge of victory.

Trades-unions represent the one effective form of combination won by American labor. Trades-unions need no timid apologists. Their vindication is in the historic tale of the successful advances which they have won for workingmen. Called into being to defend labor against legislation in the interests of capital, in the days when to ask for an advance in wages led to workingmen's being thrown into prison, they have in England led on to the brilliant series of reforms which mark our century, as told so well in the articles by Mr. Howell (*The Nineteenth Century* for October, 1882) and by Mr. Harrison (*The Contemporary Review* for October, 1883). Doubtless they have committed plenty of follies, and are still capable of stupid tyrannies that only succeed in handicapping labor, in alienating capital, and in checking producitivity—that is, in lessening the sum total of divisible wealth. Such actions are inevitable in the early stages of combination on the part of uneducated men, feeling a new sense of power, and striking blindly out in angry retaliation for real or fancied injuries.

Trades-unions are gradually, however, outgrowing their crude methods. The attempts, such as we have seen lately, of great corporations to break them up, is a piece of despotism which ought to receive an indignant rebuke from the people at large. Labor must combine, just as capital has combined, in forming these very corporations. Labor's only way of defending its interests as a class is through combination. It is the abuse and not the use of trades-unions against which resistance should be made.

The chief abuse of our trades-unions has been their concentration of attention upon the organization of strikes.

Strikes seem to me in our present stage of the "free-contract" system entirely justifiable when they are really necessary. Workingmen have the right to combine in affixing a price at which they wish to work. The supply of labor and the demand for goods, in the absence of higher considerations, will settle the question as to whether they can get the increase. The trying features of this method of reaching a result are incidental to our immature industrial system. Strikes have had their part to play in the development of that system. We note their failures and forget their successes; but they have had their signal success, and have won substantial advantages for labor. Their chief service, however, has been in teaching combination, and in showing labor the need of a better weapon by which to act than the strike itself.

The strike requires long practice and great skill to wield it well. Practice in it is more costly than the experiments at Woolwich. Mr. Dolles, in his new work on political economy, gives some statistics which abundantly illustrate the folly of strikes, although he only gives one side of the case, namely, the losses which fall directly upon the laborers themselves. If to these were added the losses of capitalists, the aggregate would become colossal. In 1829 the Manchester spinners struck, and lost $1,250,000 in wages before the dispute was at an end. The next year their brethren at Ashton and Stayleybridge followed their example in striking and in losing $1,250,000. In 1833 the builders of Manchester forfeited $360,000 by voluntary idleness. In 1836 the spinners of Preston threw away $286,000. Eighteen years afterward their successor, seventeen thousand strong, slowly starved through thirty-six weeks and paid $1,200,000 for the privilege. In 1853 the English iron-workers lost $12,000 by a strike. Such losses marked, too, the strikes of the London builders in 1860, and tailors in 1868, and the northern iron-workers in 1865. The strike of the Belfast linen-weavers, which was ended a few weeks since by the mediation of the British Association for the Advancement of Science, cost the operatives $1,000,000.

The cost of strikes is expressible only in the aggregate of the savings of labor consumed in idleness, of the loss to the productivity of the country, of the disturbance of the whole mechanism of exchange, and of the injury wrought upon the delicate social organization by the strain thus placed upon it. The famous Pittsburgh strike is estimated to have cost the country ten millions of dollars. When so costly a weapon is found to miss far more often than it hits, it is altogether too dear. * * *

Trades-unions in this country seem to me to be gravely at fault in clinging to such an obsolete weapon. They should have turned their attention to our modern improvement upon this bludgeon.

Arbitration is a far cheaper and more effective instrument of adjusting differences between capital and labor—a far more likely means of securing a fair increase of wages. It places both sides to the controversy in an amicable mood, and is an appeal to the reason and conscience—not wholly dead in the most soulless corporation. It costs next to nothing. It is already becoming a substitute for strikes in England, where the trades-unions are adopting this new weapon. * * *

Trades-unions ought, among us, to emulate the wisdom of European workingmen, and use their mechanism to organize forms of association which should look not alone to winning higher wages but to making the most of existing wages, and ultimately to leading the wage-system into a higher development. The provident features of the English trades-unions are commonly overlooked, and yet it is precisely in these provident features that their main development has been reached. Mr. George Howell shows that a number of societies, which he had specially studied, had spent in thirty years upward of $19,000,000 through their various relief-funds, and $1,369,455 only on strikes. Mr. Harrison speaks of seven societies spending in one year (1879) upward of $4,000,000 upon their members out of work. He shows that seven of the great societies spent in 1882 less than 2 per cent of their income on strikes; and states that 99 per cent of union funds in England "have been expended in the beneficent work of supporting workmen in bad times, in laying by a store for bad times, and saving the country from a crisis of destitution and strife."

Trades-unions ought to be doing for our workingmen what trades-unions have already done in England. * * * It has been by the power of combination among the workingmen, developed through the trades-unions, that this long list of beneficent legislation—factory acts, mines-regulation acts, education acts, tenant-right acts, employers' liability acts, acts against "truck," acts against cruelty to animals, etc.—has been secured. It has been wrested from reluctant parliaments by the manifestations of strength on the part of the laboring classes. * * *

Our trades unions ought to be the means of securing one of the great necessities of labor in this country—accurate and generally diffused information concerning the state of the labor-market. Were there any thorough combination in existence on the part of these unions in hard times, there could be diffused through the great centers of labor in the East regular reports of the labor-market in the different local centers of the country, such as would guide workingmen in their search for opportunities of work. * * *

Another action that our labor unions might take in the interest of the workingmen is in the development of co-operation. The story of European co-operation is one of the most encouraging tales of our modern industrial world. Germany, for example, had in 1877 some 2,830 credit societies; of which 806 reported 431,216 members; advances for the year, in loans to their members, $375,000,000, with a loss of one mark to every 416 thalers, or 23⅘ cents on every $297—an indication of soundness in their financial operations that many capitalistic corporations might well envy. The rapid growth of these societies is bringing the omnipotence of credit to the aid of the workingmen in Germany.

We have within the past decade had a most encouraging growth of a somewhat similar form of co-operation in the building and loan associations, which are now estimated to number probably about 8,000 in the nation, with a membership of 450,000, and an aggregated capital of $75,000,000.

The co-operative stores have reached a wonderful development in England, with most beneficent results. There were 765 stores reporting to the congress in 1881, which showed aggregate sales of $65,703,990, with profits of $435,000; while Scotland reported 226 stores in the same year, representing sales of $17,423,170, and profits of $113,665.

Against this showing our workingmen have comparatively little to offer. We have, it is true, had a great deal more of experimenting in co-operative distribution than is ordinarily supposed. Co-operative stores began among us between 1830 and 1840. The Workingmen's Protective Union developed a great many stores at this time, which together did a business in their best days ranging from $1,000,000 to $2,000,000 per annum. In the decade 1860–70 there was an extensive revival of co-operative stores; plans for wholesale agencies being even discussed. A few of these earlier stores still live. Two great national orders have arisen, seeking to build up co-operative stores, among other aims.

The Grangers had in 1876 twenty State purchasing agencies, three of which did a business annually of $200,000, and one of which did an annual business of $1,000,000. They claimed to have, about the same time, five steamboat or packet lines, fifty societies for shipping goods, thirty-two grain elevators, twenty-two warehouses for storing goods. In 1876 one hundred and sixty Grange stores were recorded. In he same year it was officially stated that "local stores are in successful operation all over the country."

The Sovereigns of Industry also developed co-operative distribution largely. In 1877 President Earle reported that "ninety-four councils, selected from the whole, report a membership of 7,273, and with an average capital of only $884 did a business last year of $1,089,372.55. It is safe to assume that the unreported sales will swell the amount to at least $3,000,000."

There have been numerous stores started apart from these orders. The finest success won is by the Philadelphia Industrial Co-operative Society. Starting in 1875 with one store, it has now six stores. Its sales for the quarter ending February 18, 1882, were $51,413.63. A considerable increase of interest in such stores marks the opening of our decade. Stores are starting up in various parts of the country. The Grangers claim to have now hundreds of co-operative stores, upon the Rochdale plan, in successful operation. Texas reports officially (1881) seventy-five co-operative societies connected with this order. * * *

We had an epoch of brilliant enthusiasm over co-operative agriculture in 1840–50, but little has been left from it. One form of agricultural co-operation, a lower form, has been astonishingly successful—the cheese-factories and creameries. It is estimated that there are now 5,000 of them in the country. In co-operative manufactures we have had many experiments, but few successes, from 1849 onward. Massachusetts reported twenty-five co-operative manufactories in 1875. All of them, however, were small societies.

Now, co-operation has its clearly marked limitations. It is of itself no panacea for all the ills that labor is heir to. But it can ameliorate some of the worst of those ills. It can effect great savings for our workingmen, and can secure them food and other necessaries of the best quality. If nothing further arises, the spread of co-operation may simply induce a new form of competition between these big societies; but no one can study the history of the movement without becoming persuaded that there is a moral development carried on which will, in some way as yet not seen to us, lead up the organization of those societies into some higher generalization, securing harmony. It is constantly and rightly said that business can never dispense with that which makes the secret of capital's success in large industry and trade, namely, generalship. Co-operation can, it is admitted, capitalize labor for the small industries, in which it is capable of making workingmen their own employers, but it is said it can never, through committees of management, carry on large industries or trade. I can, however, see no reason why hereafter it may not enable large associations to hire superior directing ability at high salaries, just as paid generals give to republics the leadership which kings used to supply in monarchies. There are in the savings-banks of many manufacturing centers in our country amounts which if capitalized would place the workingmen of those towns in industrial independence; moneys which, in some instances, are actually furnishing the borrowed capital for their own employers. In such towns our workingmen have saved enough to capitalize their labor, but for lack of the power of combination, let the advantage of their own thrift inure to the benefit of men already rich. They save money and then loan it to rich men to use in hiring them to work on wages, while the profits go to the borrowers of labor's savings.

But the chief value of co-operation, in my estimate, is its educating power. It opens a training school for labor in the science and art of association.

Labor once effectively united could win its dues, whatever they may be. The difficulties of such association have lain in the undeveloped mental and moral condition of the rank and file of the hosts of labor. * * *

Now, of this effort at co-operation I find scarcely any trace in the trade organizations of our workingmen. Trades-unions have until very lately passed the whole subject by in utter silence. What has been done by workingmen in this country in the line of co-operation has been done outside of the great trade associations, which form the natural instrumentalities for organizing such combination. They offer the mechanism, the mutual knowledge, the preliminary training in habits of combination, which together should form the proper conditions for the development of co-operation. Is it not a singular thing, considering the manifold benefits that would come to labor from such a development, that the attention of these great and powerful organizations has not heretofore been seriously called to this matter. * * *

The story of such attempts as have already been made in this direction is one of a sad and discouraging nature to all who feel the gravity of this problem. Again and again great organizations have risen on our soil, seeking to combine our trade associations and promising the millennium to labor, only to find within a few years suspicion, distrust, and jealousy eating the heart out of the order, and disintegration following rapidly as a natural consequence. The time must soon come let us hope, when the lesson of these experiences will have been learned.

These are some of the salient faults of labor—faults which are patent to all dispassionate observers. The first step to a better state of things lies through the correction of these faults. Whatever other factors enter into the problem, this is the factor which it concerns labor to look after if it would reach the equation of the good time coming. No reconstruction of society can avail for incompetent, indifferent, thriftless men who cannot work together. Self-help must precede all other help. Dreamers may picture utopias, where all our present laws are suspended, and demagogues may cover up the disagreeable facts of labor's own responsibility for its pitiful condition, but sensible workingmen will remember that, as Renan told his countrymen after the Franco-Prussian war, "the first duty is to face the facts of the situation." There are no royal roads to an honest mastery of fortune, though there seem to be plenty of by-ways to dishonest success. Nature is a hard school-mistress. She allows no makeshifts for the discipline of hard work and of self-denial, for the culture of all the strengthful qualities. Her American school for workers is not as yet overcrowded. The rightful order of society is not as yet submerged on our shores. There are the rewards of merit for all who will work and wait. No man of average intelligence needs to suffer in our country if he has clear grit in him. "The stone that is fit for the wall," as the Spanish proverb runs, "will not be left in the road."

II
FAULTS OF CAPITAL

But—for there is a very large "but" in the case—when all this is said, only the thorough going *doctrinaire* will fail to see that merely half the case has been presented. There is a shallow optimism which, from the heights of prosperity, throws all the blame of labor's sufferings on labor's own broad shoulders; steels the heart of society against it because of these patent faults, and closes the hand against its help, while it sings the gospel of the Gradgrinds—"As it was and ever shall be. Amen."

Labor itself is not wholly responsible for its own faults. These faults spring largely out of the defective social conditions amid which the work-ingman finds himself placed. Before we proceed to administer to him the whole measure of the "whopping" due for his low estate, we had better look back of him, to see why it is that he is as he is.

The inefficiency of labor is by no means the fault of the individual laborer alone. Heredity has bankrupted him before he started on his career. His parents were probably as inefficient as he is—and most likely *their* parents also. One who sees much of the lower grades of labor ceases to wonder why children turn out worthless, knowing what the parents were. General Francis A. Walker, in opening the Manufacturers' and Mechanics' Institute at Boston lately, said:

"There is great virtue in the inherited industrial aptitudes and instincts of the people. You can no more make a first-class dyer or a first-class machinist in one generation than you can in one generation make a Cossack horseman or a Tartar herdsman. Artisans are born, not made."

Our incompetents may plead that they were not born competent. It does not readily appear what we are going to do about this working of heredity against labor, except as by the slow and gradual improvement of mankind these low strata of existences are lifted up to a higher plane. Meanwhile we must blame less harshly and work a little more earnestly to better the human stock.

The environment of labor handicaps still further this organic deficiency. In most of our great cities the homes of the workingmen are shockingly unwholesome; unsunned, badly drained, overcrowded. The tenements of New York are enough alone to take the life out of labor. City factories often are not much better. The quality of the food sold in the poorer sections of our cities—meat, bread, milk, etc.—is defectively nutritious, even where it is not positively harmful. The sanitary conditions are thus against labor.

This could be largely reflected by the State and city authorities, and ought to be rectified in simple justice to society at large, which is now so heavily burdened by the manifold evils bred under such conditions. Government guards carefully the rights both of land and capital by an immense amount of legislation and administration. Has not labor a fair claim to an equal solicitude on the part of the State? Health is the laborer's source of wealth, but it is by no means so farefully looked after as are the resources of the other two factors of production. It is only within the last three years that in New York we have had a satisfactory tenement-house law or a fair administration of any law bearing on this evil. There ought to be the exercise of some such large wisdom as led the city of Glasgow to spend $7,000,000 in reconstructing three thousand of the worst tenements of that city, with a consequent reduction of the death rate from 54 per thousand to 29 per thousand, and with a corresponding decrease in pauperism and crime.

To this end our municipal governments should be taken out of party politics and made the corporation business that they are in German cities.

We have in none of the States of our Union any such legislation as that of the thorough system of factory laws in England, and we ought to supply the lack promptly. Whatever may be said as to interference on the part of legislation with the rights of capital, the sufficient answer is that the whole advance of society has been a constant interference on the part of legislation with the merely natural action of the law of supply and demand; and that only thus has England, for example, secured the immense amelioration in the condition of the problem of labor and capital which marks her state to-day.

It can be said also in this connection that if Government has one business more peculiarly her own than another, it is to look after the class that most needs looking after; and that not simply from the interest of the class itself, which would rarely supply a basis for governmental interference, but in the interests of society at large—of the State itself. The State's first concern is to see her citizens healthful, vigorous, wealth-producing factors; and to this end bad sanitary conditions, which undermine the "health-capital" of labor, imperatively demand correction.

The deeper seated the roots of labor's inefficiency in heredity and environment, the greater the need for an education that will develop whatever potencies may lie latent. Inefficiency will rarely correct itself. Superior ability must train it into better power. Where is there any proper provision for such an education?

State governments and our National Government have for a number of years been fostering certain branches of industrial education, chiefly in the line of agriculture. The late report of the Bureau of Education upon industrial education presents a very encouraging summary of what is thus being done under the guidance of the State. It reports concerning forty-three colleges aided by State grants to give agricultural and mechanical training, besides a large number of technical departments in other colleges, industrial schools, evening classes for such instruction, etc. Probably the finest example of industrial education that the country possesses is found in the Hampton schools in Virginia. Of attempts, however, to combine general and intellectual education with practical training and handicrafts we have few examples. The Hampton schools, already alluded to, present one of the best. Professor Adler's school in this city is very interesting in this respect.

Our common schools have until lately signally passed by the whole field of practical education. Drawing is at last being generally introduced, and sewing is also being introduced to a small extent, I believe, especially in New England. But the schools which are supposed to be intended for the mass of the people, and which are supplied at the public cost, have made next to no provision for the practiced training of boys and girls to become self-supporting men and women—wealth-producing citizens; while the whole curriculum of the school-system tends to a disproportionate intellectuality, and to an alienation from all manual labor. * * *

The necessity of the State's entering the educational field is disputed by no one; but if it is to educate children at the public cost it is bound, I think, to so educate its wards that they shall return to society the taxation imposed for their education. Its justification in becoming school-master lies in the necessity of making out of the raw material of life citizens who shall be productive factors in the national wealth and conservators of its order. If, therefore, it is justified in teaching the elementary branches of education, if it is justified in adding to those elementary branches departments that may be considered in the nature of luxuries, how much more is it justified in training the powers by which self-support shall be won and wealth shall be added to society! * * *

That such efforts to encourage industrial education would pay our Government is best seen in the example of England. The International Exhibition of 1851 revealed to England its complete inferiority to several continental countries in art-industries, and the cause of that inferiority in the absence of skilled workmen. The Government at once began to study the problem, and out of this study arose the Kensington Museum, with its art-schools, and similar institutions throughout the country, which have already made quick and gratifying returns in the improvement of the national art-industries, and in the vast enrichment of the trade growing therefrom.

Concerning the uninterestedness of labor and its too common lack of any identification with capital, we must also look beyond labor itself to find the full responsibility of this evil.

The whole condition of industrial labor has changed in our century. Contrast the state of such labor a century ago with what it is now. Then the handicraftsman worked in his own home, surrounded by his family, upon a task all the processes of which he had mastered, giving him thus a sense of interest and pride in the work being well and thoroughly done.

Now he leaves his home early and returns to it late, working during the day in a huge factory with several hundred other men. The subdivision of labor gives him now only a bit of the whole process to do, where the work is still done by hand, whether it be the making of a shoe or a piano. He cannot be master of a craft, but only master of a fragment of the craft. He cannot have the pleasure or pride of the old-time workman, for he *makes* nothing. He sees no complete product of his skill growing into finished shape in his hands. What zest can there be in this bit of manhood? Steam machinery is slowly taking out of his hands even this fragment of intelligent work, and he is set at feeding and watching the great machine which has been endowed with the brains that once were in the human toiler. Man is reduced to being the tender upon a steel automaton which thinks and plans and combines with marvelous power, leaving him only the task of supplying it with the raw material, and of oiling and cleansing it.

Some few machines require a skill and judgment to guide them proportioned to their own astonishing capacities, and for the elect workmen who manage and guide them there is a new sense of the pleasure of power.

But, for the most part, mechanism takes the life out of labor as the handicraft becomes the manufacture—or, more properly, the *machino*-facture; and the problem of to-day is, how to keep up the interest of labor in its daily task, from which the zest has been stolen.

Manufacturers ought to see this problem and hasten to solve it. Those who profit most by the present factory system ought, in all justice, to be held responsible to those who suffer most from it. They ought to be held morally bound to make up to them in some way the interest in life that has gone out with the old handicrafts. They could interest their hands *out* of the working hours, and in ways that would give them a new interest *in* their working hours. * * *

Not a few of our manufacturers are already opening their eyes to the facts of the industrial problem, and, with far-seeing generosity and human brotherliness that will, according to the eternal laws, return even the good things of this world unto them, they are providing their workingmen with libraries, reading-rooms, and halls for lectures and entertainments. They are encouraging and stimulating the formation of literary and debating societies, bands, and clubs, and such other things as give social fellowship and mental interest. All this can be done at comparatively small cost. The men in the employ of a great establishment can be taught a new interest in their task as they learn to understand its processes and the relation of these processes to society at large, which can easily be done by lectures, etc. Such work as this is a work that demands the leadership, the organizing power, which the employer can best furnish. At the last session of the Social Science Association an interesting paper sketched some of these efforts. In what wiser way could our wealthy manufacturers use a portion of the money won for them by the labor which has exhausted its own interest in its task?

Such personal interest on the part of employers in their employees leads up to a clue to that other branch of the uninterestedness of labor—its lack of identification with the welfare of capital—its lack of any feeling of loyalty toward the capitalist. How can anything else be fairly expected in our present state of things from the *average* workingman under the *average* employer? I emphasize the "average" because there are employees of exceptional intelligence and honor, as there are employers of exceptional conscientiousness, anxious to do fairly by their men. The received political economy has taught the average workingman that the relations of capital and labor are those of hostile interests; that profits and wages are in an inverse ratio; that the symbol of the factory is a see-saw, on which capital goes up as labor goes down. As things are, there is unfortunately too much ground for this notion, as the workman sees.

Mr. Carroll D. Wright, in the fourteenth annual report of the Massachusetts Bureau of Labor (1883), shows that in 1875 the percentage of wages paid to the value of production, in over 2,000 establishments, was 24.68; and that in 1880 it was 20.23. This means that the workingmen's share of the returns of their own labor, so far from increasing, has decreased one sixth in five years.

The workingman is disposed to believe in the light of such figures that the large wealth accumulated by his employer represents over and above a fair profit the increased wages out of which he naturally regards himself as being mulcted. He may be thick-headed, but he can see that in such a see-saw of profits *versus* wages the superior power of capital has the odds all in its favor. He learns to regard the whole state of the industrial world as one in which *might* makes *right,* and feebleness is the synonym of fault.

How, in the name of all that is reasonable, can the average man take much interest in his employer or identity himself with that employer under such a state of things as the economy sanctioned by the employer has taught him? This is aggravated by the whole character of our modern industrial system.

The factory system is a new feudalism, in which a master rarely deals directly with his hands. Superintendents, managers, and "bosses" stand between him and them. He does not know them; they do not know him. The old common feeling is disappearing. And—this is a significant point that it behooves workingmen to notice—the intermediaries are generally workingmen who have risen out of the ranks of manual labor and have lost all fellow-feeling with their old comrades, without gaining the larger sympathy with humanity which often comes from better culture. The hardest men upon workingmen are ex-workingmen. It is stated, on what seems to be good authority, that the general superintendent of the great corporation which lately has shown so hard a feeling towards its operatives when on a strike was himself only ten years ago a telegraph-operator.

A further aggravating feature of this problem is the increasing tendency of capital to associated action. What little knowledge of his employees or sympathy with them the individual manufacturer might have is wholly lost in the case of the corporation. To the stockholders of a great joint-stock company, many of whom are never on the spot, the hundreds of laborers employed by the company are simply "hands"—as to whose possession of hearts or minds or souls the by-laws rarely take cognizance. Here there is plainly a case where capital—the party of brains and wealth —the head of the industrial association, should lead off in a systematic effort and renew, as far as may be, the old human tie, for which no substitute has ever been devised.

To conciliate the interests of the classes, and identify labor with capital, individual employers must re-establish personal relationships between themselves and their men. What might be done in this way, and how, this being done, the present alienation of feeling on the part of our workingmen would largely disappear, must be evident to any one who has watched some of the beautiful exemplifications of this relationship which have already grown into being on our shores. I know of one large manufacturer, in a city not a hundred miles from this, who started to enter the ministry as a young man, but found to his intense disappointment that he had no aptitude for the work of a preacher, and turned his attention, on the insistent advice of those nearest to him, to active business. He took up the business which his father had left him at his death and had left largely involved. His first task was to pay off, dollar for dollar, all the debts which his father had bequeathed him, although in most instances they had been compromised by his creditors. He then threw the energy of his being into development of the business, and, in the course of a few years, put it at the forefront of that line in his native city. Into his business he breathed the spirit of love to God and man which had moved him originally to take up the work of the ministry. He felt himself ordained to be what Carlyle would have called a "captain of industry." From the start he established personal, human, living relationships with his men. He taught them by deed rather than by word to consider him their friend. He was in the habit of calling in upon their families in a social and respecting way. In all their troubles and adversities he trained them to counsel with him, and gave them the advantage of his riper judgment and larger vision. In cases of exigency his means were at their service in the way of loans to tide them over the hard times. His friends have seen, more than once, coming from his private office some of the hard-fisted men of toil in his employ, with tears streaming down their faces. He had called them into the office on hearing of certain bad habits into which they had fallen, and so impressive had been his talk with them, that they left his presence with the most earnest resolves to do better in the future. The result of all this relationship has been that during some fifteen years of the management of this large business he has rarely changed his men, and while strikes have abounded around him he has never known a strike.

I hold in my possession a letter from one of our leading iron-manufacturers in this country, who, in response to an appeal for participation in a charity of this city, gave answer that it had been a practice of the firm to invest a certain portion of their profits in developing the comforts of their workingmen, and that they were obliged to limit their desire to give in charity in order that they might be able to build homes, club-rooms, reading-rooms, and all the *et ceteras* of a really civilized community in their work-village. These are examples, in our own country, of what might be done.

One of the most beautiful models that I know of in modern history is furnished by the town to which reference has already been made—the town of Mulhouse, where, after some thirty years, the spirit of brotherliness has so entered into the relationships of capital and labor that a firm would be disreputable which there attempted to carry on business as business is ordinarily done here. All the manufacturers plan out, organize, and carry on what to most of us would seem impossible schemes for the amelioration and uplifting of the condition of their working people. No one wonders that, as he walks through the town which his large hearted philanthropy imbued with this fine spirit, the workingmen salute the originator of these schemes as "Father Peter."

In addition to this personal, human relationship, capital might and should, in all justice and humanity, identify the pecuniary interests of labor with its own interests. What is known as industrial partnership is simply a solution of this branch of the problem. The principle is simply that of giving labor a pecuniary interest in the profits of the establishment *pro rata* with his own wages. A *bonus* is set on frugality and industry and conscientiousness of work by making the hands small partners in the concern. * * *